—About growing up in a warm and wonderful family, and in a town where to be soft was to be crushed

—About learning about sex from a high school teacher in a tender, deeply touching affair

—About becoming a college All-American while refusing to talk to his coaches

—About watching his brother crack up and come back in pursuit of an athletic career

—About players he worshipped, like Bobby Layne, players he feared, like Big Daddy Lipscomb, and the men with the money whom he learned to hate

—About being suspended from football for a year—how it happened and why it still makes him mad

—About the last glory years and what it felt like to get the final ax

—About movies and TV and Howie Cosell

An athlete grows old. A man grows up. And Alex Karras has written about it all.

"Not the usual athlete's autobiography, but of course Alex Karras is no ordinary jock."—ST. LOUIS POST-DISPATCH

"Funny, tender, and brutally honest!"
—ASSOCIATED PRESS

"A delight . . . ribald humor . . . savvy . . . honesty."—TAMPA TRIBUNE

Other Sports Books from SIGNET

EVEN BIG GUYS CRY

❧

Alex Karras
with Herb Gluck

Ⓢ
A SIGNET BOOK
NEW AMERICAN LIBRARY
TIMES MIRROR

1. A Lucky Breeze Blew

"Hey, Alex; tell us a story. . . ."

Okay. Let's begin with this. It's summertime and I'm driving up to the ultraposh Houston Country Club in a woolly red hunting jacket, Levis, rubber boots, and a squirrel cap with side flaps covering the ears. Understand I'm also in a Land Rover that's been gushing around in the mud all day. So heads are turned to see what the hell went by.

I come to a halt at the front entrance and the doorman peers at me through his monocle. "You must be somewhat off the beaten path," he says. Then he gets ready to blow his little silver whistle. I can't stand the sound of whistles—never have—so I climb out of my vehicle and pull it from his mouth. Which brings on the security cops, and pretty soon we're all in an uproar. Fortunately, the club's entertainment director breaks through and yells, "Let him in! He's making a speech!"

That's me. Alex Karras. The pudgy-nosed, tippy-toed pixie of your television tube, big picture screen, and party-time soirees. Today it's a speech in Houston. Tomorrow I'm acting in a Hollywood movie . . . working with Howard Cosell and Frank Gifford on a "Monday Night Football" telecast in Cincinnati . . . flying to New York for a series of commercials. . . . It's a great life. A barrel of laughs. I don't ever want it to end.

But everything does. Even the most beautiful dreams. You wake up and—poof—they're gone; soap bubbles popping in the wind.

Dreams. And thoughts tumbling back in time ...

In 1958 I was an All-America tackle from the University of Iowa and a number-one draft choice of the Detroit Lions. Through the spring and early summer of that year I eagerly waited for training camp to open. I would be meeting Bobby Layne, Hopalong Cassady, Jim David, Joe Schmidt, Lou Creekmur, Jack Christiansen, Yale Lary—guys who had contributed heavily in the Lion drive to a 1957 National Football League championship. More than anything, I wanted to play in Detroit and be on a winning team.

Wishes and dreams. Certainly, a few of them were realized during thirteen roller-coaster seasons in Detroit. Altogether, I left the game with more than a thousand jokes and stories to tell. Enough to get me into show business. Enough to write a book. I'm grateful for all that. Football doesn't owe me a thing.

It gave me goals to shoot for. The nearest one to my heart—to be the best defensive tackle in the NFL. As a schoolkid, I'd walk down the block and, invariably, someone would say, "There goes Lou Karras's little brother." Louie had made it to the Washington Redskins by then. I knew it would take a tremendous effort to fill his shoes. In my mind, the only way to do it was to be the greatest football player who ever lived.

Speaking of shoes, my brother Teddy loaned me the only good pair he had, so I could graduate public school looking halfway decent. That's the way I grew up, trying to be just like Louie and Teddy, and living in hand-me-downs.

I dress kinda funky today. Out here in Southern California, where I live, I feel more comfortable in a pair of jeans and a T-shirt than in a Pierre Cardin suit.

This is not to say I go out looking like a bum. A few snappy numbers are hanging in my closet right now. I wear them to all the proper places. The important thing is, now that I can afford to dress any way I want, I still think of the days when I ran around the streets of Gary in a pair of flapping shoes. So, if the clothes are clean—and they're mine—I'm not going to worry about what the other guy thinks.

What boils me is that in every phase of our "free enterprise" system people in high positions are constantly prepared to shoot down anyone who expresses an independent thought. It's certainly true in professional football. If a player stands up and says boo, chances are he's going to be in some sort of trouble with the front office. "Take that man away, he's a kook," says a coach. "Our values are being threatened," says an owner. Well, what the hell is that? I've seen some of the nicest, most dedicated athletes in this country get cut up and thrown to the wolves just because they dared to state a fresh idea or have a different opinion.

It's the old saw, I guess. *Don't bite the hand that feeds you.* Pro football owners would love to have that line included in every player's contract.

There were instances, as a matter of fact, when this kind of mentality placed heavy pressure on a number of sportswriters and broadcasters in the field. It came in the form of direct or indirect payola. Reporters who presented a favorable image of club policy were taken care of. Those who reported flaws in the system usually found themselves on the outside looking in.

Remember, there are twenty-eight teams in the National Football League today; all of them are run by influential businessmen. In some cases, football is their play toy. The jackpot dollars come from other sources —banks, insurance firms, motion-picture companies, huge conglomerates, and so on. You name it, chances are they either own it outright or have a good piece of the action. And the bigger they are the more influence they command.

An example. In the late sixties, Al Ackerman, then a sportscaster with WWJ-TV in Detroit, had been taking terrific shots at Lion owner Bill Ford, telling his viewers the truth about what was really going on in the organization. Bad trades, senseless cuts, inept management—all the things that prevented the Lions from becoming a first-rate power in the NFL Western Conference. So what happened? Ackerman was summoned to his general manager's office and told that because Bill Ford happened to be a member of the Ford Motor Company family, the station would not play Russian roulette with the account. Undeterred, Ackerman went right back to his microphone and continued to blast away. It wasn't long before he was out on the street looking for another job.

Let's turn the coin. In 1963, the blackest year of my professional life, the politics of broadcast journalism hit home where I least expected it. In the heart.

A radio sports announcer with a big following in the Detroit area liked to gamble. So did I. During my first few years as a Lion we got to know each other rather well. I looked upon him as a friend, as someone I could depend on. One day he came to me and said he desperately needed money. Would I give him some inside information on an upcoming game? He was laying down a big bet and couldn't afford to get in any deeper with his bookie. I told him exactly what I knew. No more or less than what any fan gets out of his daily newspaper or weekly tout sheet. Whether he won the bet is of little consequence. But it hurt like hell when he turned on me in his broadcasts after my suspension for betting on NFL games. Dollars to doughnuts he was pressured to. His station carried all our games.

Well, that was fourteen years ago. Times have changed. Today, few owners exert even the slightest pressure on writers and broadcasters to slant stories favorably for their teams. They're no longer wined and dined, accommodated in the best hotels, or sent off on fancy vacations free of charge. Now it's a hot dog, a beer, and thank you very much.

Times change, all right. So, inevitably, I've changed. At a younger age, I kept wondering why there was so much meanness in this world. Where excellence was supposed to be found in leadership, in many cases I saw nothing but mediocrity. When that happened, it became difficult to contain myself. I would sulk, or grit my teeth and pray that I wouldn't lose my temper. But the violence came spilling out a couple of times. I don't defend it. Not any more. But it had to run its course. I knew of no other way to express my rage.

During college, one incident had me so wrought up I wanted to kick goal posts loose, tear apart blocking dummies, smash locker doors, do *anything* to get rid of the frustration. I was kidding myself. All the pent-up hostility centered on my head coach. So I had a showdown with him. He came *this* close to being strangled to death.

I remember happier times. In 1958 a lucky breeze blew, the tide rose, and George Wilson came into my life. I've never met anyone quite like him. What a tremendous man!

He was one of the original "Monsters of the Midway" as an end with the Chicago Bears. His greatest moment as a player? No, it wasn't a sensational catch to win a ball game. According to Wilson, during a game against the Washington Redskins in 1940 he threw a block against two defensive players and sprung his halfback loose for a 68-yard touchdown run.

Later he became an assistant under Bear owner-coach George Halas, then understudied Bo McMillin and Buddy Parker at Detroit. In 1957, his first year as head coach, Wilson won a league title.

I guess he knew the game as thoroughly as anyone. But he had something else that counted. You couldn't find it in his X's and O's on the blackboard, or in the way he sent men off the bench during a crucial game. What he had was this great ability to empathize with any player who came to him with a problem. A rarity among coaches then, a rarity today.

Oh, he had his faults. He could be tough and mean, could kick ass if he had to. And there wasn't a man alive who could outcuss him when things went wrong on the practice field. But he forgave and forgot. Wilson never looked at pro football as the most important thing in life. He lived by higher feelings and emotions, standards that, to my way of thinking, made him one of the most beautiful guys in the world.

Let me tell you a story about how Wilson and I got together.

It starts with a long drive from the College All-Star camp at Evanston, Illinois, in the late summer of 1958. Wayne Walker and I are on our way to Cranbrook, the Detroit preseason camp near Bloomfield Hills, Michigan; Wayne, the Lions' number-four draft pick, is behind the wheel of his beat-up Chevy.

It's way past midnight. I'm hunched up in the back seat, thinking terrible thoughts. I can still hear Otto Graham, the All-Star coach, calling me a loafer, a troublemaker. "You'll never make it in the NFL," he's saying. "Karras, you've got the worst attitude I've ever seen in a ballplayer."

The words are like a death sentence. They go round and round in my head. They come out cold and unbending. In a panic, I suddenly tap Wayne on the shoulder.

"Hey, maybe we ought to wait until morning. Nobody's going to be up to greet us, anyway."

"Hang in, Al. We're getting close."

A few minutes later Wayne pulls up alongside the rookie barracks. We get out of the car, then creep up the stairs to the top floor. Wayne finds his room. I'm left in the hall with a bunch of dive-bombing mosquitoes. By now all I want to do is get the hell out of camp, give up everything I've ever worked for, and go home. But the thought is lost in my utter exhaustion, which is helped along by sounds of snoring and grunting coming from my room. I tiptoe in and find myself looking down on a young guy like myself: crew-cut hair, baby-faced, big, and heavy. Just then, he starts blasting away in his bed from both ends. I figure the guy's a linebacker.

There's a knock on the door. It's George Wilson. "Out here," he says. Like a forlorn pup, I follow him down the hall.

"I have a report from Otto Graham about you," says Wilson with a whiskey breath that can peel paint. "It's awful. As a matter of fact, he thinks you're not going to make it here. What do you have to say for yourself?"

In the dimness I find Wilson's eyes.

"I've been through these things many times in my life, coach. I hope you'll give me a chance, that's all."

"Well, Alex, I want to tell you exactly how I feel. If Otto Graham says that about you—you must be one *great* sonofabitch. I'm glad to have you here."

We shake hands, and Wilson goes down the stairs

singing a chorus of "When They Cut Down the Ol'
Pine Tree."

So much to remember. The coach, those ballplayers, that camp—I see the first day of practice as
though I'm there now.

"Listen, you rookie punk . . ." one guy growls.
And two guys hammer me.

"You four-eyed punk rookie creep!" yells another.
And the side of a wall falls on my head.

I get up grinning. "Fuck you guys! I'm gonna be
here long after you're gone!"

Memories. Before the machine took over. Before
that, I see a shaft of pure daylight, and a stampede of
bodies; strong and supple youngsters moving along
the grass of a dozen NFL stadiums, heads down, legs
churning toward a distant goal. I see Wayne Walker,
Kenny Russell, Kar Koepfer, Dave Whitsell, Jim
Gibbons, and Bill Glass . . . all eager rookies like
myself. We're ready to compete against the fastest,
toughest players in the professional ranks.

I   see   Layne,   Creekmur,   David,   Cassady
Christiansen . . . and Jim Martin, Tobin Rote, John
Henry Johnson, Jim Moran—the oldest veterans of the
1958 Lion squad. Gil Mains is there, too. A defensive
tackle. I'm after his job. He's going to fight hard to
hang on to it. Mains has been sweating and pushing
and damn near killing himself since high school so he
can stay in the pit for just one more season—and the
season after that. Forget the past, never mind what's
already been accomplished. It's all reduced to one
thing: perform like a champion, or make way for a
new one.

Well, you better watch out, Gil Mains. There's a
new kid on the block who's gonna stick it to you. It's

me, Alex Karras, the greatest defensive tackle in the whole wide world.

That's what I saw during my first year in the pros. I watched the Lions give everything they had to give. Not only for money or for fame, but for something much deeper. A love for the game itself. And all the players in the league, from the brightest stars to the most obscure substitutes, played with equal devotion to the cause.

Big Daddy Lipscomb played like that.

He arrived in the NFL without a college education, right out of the Detroit sandlots to a berth on the Los Angeles Rams in 1953. Three years later he went over to the Baltimore Colts, then joined the Pittsburgh Steelers in 1961. In the spring of 1963, at the age of thirty-one, they found him dead on the sidewalk in front of a Baltimore hospital. An official coroner's report confirmed an overdose of hard drugs. Yet the people who knew him best claimed that Big Daddy never took dope in his life, that he must've been injected by someone he didn't know. Whatever the circumstances, it was a sad day when he passed from the scene.

My own recollection of Lipscomb is vivid. He had to be the most intimidating figure in pro football history. I never could see too well without my glasses, but, on or off, the mere sight of him quickened my heartbeat, set the adrenaline flowing, and made me take off in the opposite direction. I'd take an oath on it—the man stood seven foot nine, weighed 8,217 pounds, breathed fire, and farted the same way.

All of which means that ballplayers were scared out of their shoes when he showed up for a game. Especially the guys who had to play against him. Opposing linemen called him "sir," and asked about his family, his dog, and how things were going at home.

Once in a while, this helped to ease Lipscomb into a docile state, but not for long. He had this peculiar fetish, this basic instinct that separated him from all other defensive tackles in the NFL. *He came out to kill you!*

Which reminds me of still another story. My one and only confrontation with Big Daddy on a football field.

We're playing the Steelers in a home opener, and our offense had all its guns going early in the first quarter. I'm watching it all from the sideline, with particular emphasis on Big Daddy, who's showing me moves that I've never before seen by a defensive tackle. He probably woke up in a bad mood this morning, because the dirt is flying in his vicinity and our guards are coming out of it like drunks being tossed from a saloon. Anyway, we finally get into field-goal position. George Wilson sends in Wayne Walker to try one from 32 yards out. Then he decides to send me in to block on the line. This never happened before, so I run up to Wilson and say, "I'm *defense*, coach. You sure you want me out there?"

"On the double, Karras!"

I move to the guard position, which puts me directly in front of Big Daddy. Squatting down to face him, I see his lips fold back. Steam escapes from his mouth. "Ah'm gonna kill you," he says.

A few seconds later, Walker puts his toe into the ball. Big Daddy shoots up from the ground, deflects the kick, knocks me down, and grinds his foot into my ass three times. I get up and say, "Thank you, Big Daddy," and stagger off the field.

Next thing I know, our premier quarterback, Milt Plum, engineers a touchdown drive that brings forty-five thousand fans up off their seats. Once again Wilson sends me in, this time to block for the extra point.

Sure enough, Big Daddy proceeds to beat the living shit out of me just like before, and I thank him kindly for doing such a swell job of it.

It goes on like this all afternoon. We keep on scoring touchdowns and I keep getting it from Big Daddy. On our fourth scoring play, Lipscomb gets so incensed he removes my helmet, hits me over the head with it, and almost buries me in the ground. Right then and there I make a vow that if this stupid quarterback of ours throws one more touchdown pass, I'll find a way to get thrown out of the game.

Wouldn't you know, Plum immediately gets back in the groove. He marches straight down the field on the strength of his arm for a fifth touchdown. And I go in again for the extra point. The count's set on four. I take off on two, punch Big Daddy on the mouth as hard as I can, and step back. He blinks, then snorts. The guy isn't human.

In desperation, I grab the referee and stick him between me and Big Daddy.

"Hey, ref, didn't you see what I just did? I not only jumped offside, I hit Lipscomb right in the face, which is a violation of rule number seven. You have to kick me out of the game. I want to leave right now!"

"I didn't see it," says the referee.

"Well, you better take my word for it. That's what I did. So kick me out of the fucking game."

Meanwhile, Big Daddy is kicking clumps of grass out of the turf like a crazed bull. This upsets the official, so he pipes up, "Okay, Karras, you're out of the game."

Feeling safe and home free, I beeline it to the sideline, but not before turning around to sing out, "Hey, Big Daddy, I don't know who you think you are, but I'm the toughest sonofabitch to ever come out of

Gary, Indiana. If I ever catch you off the field, I'm gonna whip your ass!"

The man is three stories higher than me. As I look at him, his eyes are absolutely on fire.

About an hour later I'm back in my hotel. The phone rings; someone confirming a business appointment at a downtown restaurant. I get dressed up, then leave the room, whistling all the way to the elevator.

The numbers descend: 22, 21, 20, 19 . . . then stop. The doors open, and the wildest, meanest-looking guy I've ever seen in my entire life gets in. It's Big Daddy.

Immediately I remove my glasses, bow my head, and don't say a word. In total silence, we ride down to the lobby. Just as I'm getting out, feeling sure that Lipscomb hasn't recognized me, a huge paw clamps down on my shoulder.

"I know who the fuck you are, Karras."

Without missing a beat I say, "Big Daddy, have you read your NFL player's contract?"

"Naw . . ."

"Well, if you look at your contract, you'll see we have just added a clause that says we're all union brothers. And as union brothers we have to stick together, no matter what."

"Yeah?"

"That's right. By the way, do you know the union song?"

"Fuck no."

"Well, you better learn it."

I leave him there, scratching his head, and hope I never run into him again.

I never did.

2. Shadow and Light

I was born in Gary, Indiana, on July 15, 1935. My father was a doctor in that town. For nearly twenty years he treated working-class people in a dingy office on Broadway, one flight above a second-rate movie theater. At night he'd often be roused from sleep by a frantic phone call. Sometimes I'd hear him: a rasping cough, footsteps down the hall, the sound of bottles and instruments clicking inside a leather satchel. Sometimes I'd wake up to see clouds of black smoke rise in the early morning sky and know my father wasn't in his bed.

He came to America in 1902 with my grandparents, and was delivered from the steerage of a refugee ship to Ellis Island. A new beginning. And for my grandfather, a resolve never to return to his native Athens—no matter what. Back there, he grew up in a beautiful house. He had a sloping lawn to play on. Private teachers instructed him in music and art. A staff of servants catered to his every whim. He had everything an upper-class child could wish for. But at age nineteen grandpa eloped with the cook's daughter. Disinherited, forced to discontinue his law studies at the university, he found work as a dishwasher and part-time waiter. When my grandmother became pregnant, he decided to leave the country. Three years later, Louis and Sophie Karras, and their three-year-old son, George, sailed from Athens. There wasn't a spare dime in my grandfather's pocket. But when he touched American soil for the first time, he felt like the richest man alive.

The truth of it is that material wealth eluded his grasp. Life, with all its disappointments, ended for him in an agonizing sigh some forty years after he had left his homeland. Yet, my earliest recollection of him is one of comfort and well-being. He gave me that at a time when the outside world—beyond the neighborhood—seemed awfully scary. Maybe that's why I held on to my baby bottle until I was seven. Maybe that's why I spent so many hours in my grandfather's room.

Bang! Bang! My mother at his door.

"What . . . what?" grandpa grumbles, as if awakened from a sound sleep.

"Is Alex in there with his bottle?"

"No bottle. He's sleeping. I'm sleeping. Go away."

That's the way it was. We understood each other. And I wanted to be just like him.

One morning he carried me to the market on his broad shoulders. As he strutted through the crowded stalls, singing loudly in Greek, I started to copy him, mimicking the words, then gesturing broadly as though I were an opera singer taking curtain bows. The act went over big. "Ah, good," he said. "Everybody in America likes the Greeks."

Well, grandpa didn't like New York. He left it shortly after getting off the boat. "Bad times," he said. "No work. So grandma, your papa, and me—we go to Chicago. Plenty of work in Chicago."

That was in 1903. My grandparents lived on Halsted Street, in the Greek section of the city. A noisy, bustling community of bedraggled storefronts and faded red-brick houses. Grandpa worked in that neighborhood for a long time. The highest position he ever held was that of night watchman.

My father worked from the time he was in high

school. For a couple of summers he clerked at the Atlas Grocery Company. A number of years ago, when the Lions were in Chicago for a game, I visited the place. His old boss was still there. We sat around, talking a little football and a whole lot about my father.

He went to the University of Chicago as a premedical student. At six-two, weighing about 235 pounds, he could have played football under head coach Alonzo Stagg. But he didn't have any time for athletics. He wanted to be a doctor. A nobler profession he couldn't imagine. So, after completing his studies at the university, he attended medical school at the Dalhousie Hospital in Halifax, Nova Scotia. There, he met a registered nurse by the name of Emmiline Wilson. Canadian-born, of Scotch-Irish descent, my mother was then a tall, shapely girl with big blue eyes, long blonde hair, and a flawless complexion. The first time dad laid eyes on her she was standing behind a glass partition that faced one of the wards. He looked up from a chart, smiled, and she opened the diet-kitchen door to let him in.

"May I have a glass of water?" he asked. "I think my duodenal ulcer is acting up."

They were married on October 18, 1926. Two years later they moved to Gary, Indiana.

Before the turn of this century, Gary was a wasteland of dunes and marshes on the southern shore of Lake Michigan. In 1901 industrial progress created a boom town. Factories went up. Molten steel poured from huge blast furnaces. Smokestacks belched flame and soot into the sky. An army of laborers gasped for air as they sweated from dawn to dusk, and nobody complained. Instead, they paid homage to the town's benefactor, Judge Elbert H. Gary, chairman of the board of United States Steel.

In the next decade USS was joined by other manufacturers. They built giant foundries, too. They beat out the stuff and substance that molded the face of twentieth-century America. By 1929 virtually every family had a father, son, or brother working in the mills. In those circumstances, my father came to Gary to look around for a place to set up a practice. By then, my brother Louie had been born.

GEORGE KARRAS, M.D. The shingle hung outside his office in downtrodden Indiana Harbor. What an office! Two tiny rooms above a confectionery store. And one of them served as an apartment for our family.

Indiana Harbor is about ten minutes from the center of Gary. It lies in the shadow of the enormous tankers and other transports that line up regularly to carry coke, gas, tin, and steel to all parts of the world. There, for as long as I can remember, Slavs, Greeks, Italians, southern blacks, and Mexicans bent their backs to an honest living. The Mexicans were at the bottom of the work ladder. In order to understand their language, my father attended night school, then listened as they told him about their work at the mills and loading docks. Their desperate stories explained why so many of them had respiratory diseases, and wicked burns and broken bones suffered through careless accidents.

Within a year my father had established himself with the poor. He was a good guy, they said. He didn't overcharge; in fact, he seldom asked for a fee. He seemed to know who could pay and who couldn't.

With the birth of my sister, Helene, in 1930, living conditions in the tiny office-apartment became unbearable. So my father found a three-bedroom apartment in Westside Gary, in a substantial, wood-frame colonial house on Adams Street. Our landlord, a portly, jovial Greek by the name of Zacaliras, lived on the ground floor.

Mr. Zacaliras also owned a large commercial building on Broadway, the main business street of Gary. In this building, he ran the Mayflower Restaurant and collected rent from the Grand Theatre and a dozen professional offices on the second floor. My father rented one of the offices.

The remaining four Karras children were born while my parents lived on Adams Street. Nick arrived in 1931. Teddy was born two years later. I followed Teddy by sixteen months. And our baby brother, Paulie, came along in 1937.

Shadow and light: A day in winter, cold and uninviting. I'm four years old, bundled up for the outdoors. I begin to count: "One . . . two . . ." The snow calls, mounds of puffy snow calling for me to join my brothers in a sleigh ride. "Three . . . four . . ." Headfirst I tumble down down down the remaining steps, like a rock falling from a jagged cliff. My mother runs from the kitchen, screaming. She picks me up. "Are you all right?" I nod. There is no pain. Only fright. "Next time be careful."

In the snow I look for my brothers. Louie waves. He comes toward me, pulling Nick and Teddy along on his Flexible Flyer sled.

"Looo-eeeee! I want a ride!"

A summer night. I wake up, sweating. Heat rolls in through the open window, choking-hot and burning with soot from the mills. It's dark; the bed is wet. Teddy stirs in his sleep, then turns over. I shake Paulie.

"Did you pee?"

He whimpers and kicks his feet in protest. So I climb over Teddy and Paulie and stagger to the other bed, where Louie and Nick are sleeping. The sheets are dry, but the air smells of urine.

Adams Street is where I live and play. I never go beyond its corners. One day, acting out a fantasy, I venture forth on a tricycle, with Paulie perched on the back. We spin around the block. Broadway springs up like magic. The tricycle moves past the stores and pool rooms and movie houses, and the Lake Hotel, and the Mayflower Restaurant; we are weaving and bobbing through the crowds like a cork in a gentle current. Time slows.

"Where's Paulie?" my mother asks when I get home. I don't know. So my mother puts me across her knee and pounds away. Then she drags me back to Broadway and into all the stores, as though I were a rag doll. "Have you seen my little boy?" she asks the people.

We find Paulie in Woolworth's, eating a double-dip ice-cream cone. A man in a blue uniform holds Paulie on his lap. He's the first policeman I've ever seen.

I'm five, and in Jefferson grade school. We have a rest period. The teacher marches us to the gymnasium. Mats are on the floor. "All right, children. Lie down and go to sleep."

I don't want to. I stand while the other children curl up on their kindergarten beds. The teacher stares at me. "Why aren't you taking your nap?"

No answer. I sink down on the mat. For a whole hour I lie there and wonder why God made me so big. The other kids fit. Why can't I?

Why?

Spring morning. My cousin and godmother, Mary Kalaris, is getting married. My mother dresses me in a blue wool suit with grown-up pants. We're going to

Chicago for Mary's wedding. We pile into my father's car and I wave good-bye to Adams Street and Broadway, and look out the window as we ride past the mills. I see men walk into clouds of steam and disappear.

In Chicago I see a swirling of skirts and people dancing in circles. Music shakes the hall. There are fiddles and drums, an accordion, and a blaring trumpet. There's clapping and stamping of feet and heat and long white tables of food and wine, and everybody is laughing. My father gets up and sings in Greek. He has a beautiful voice. The people cheer. They come over and shake his hand and hug his neck. He smiles. I see that his face is red from the Greek wine. And he looks handsome in his shiny black tuxedo. He dances with my mother. Everybody else steps back and beats on the floor with their heels as my father and mother whirl around and around the floor. I sit at a table with my brothers and sister and watch it all. My head swims.

It's night. The car drives through wide dark streets. I see the tall buildings of Chicago climb into the sky like lighted Christmas trees. I fall asleep looking at the lights.

Winter night. I'm in bed, sick with fever. My father comes into the room, slope-shouldered and weary-eyed. Melting snowflakes glisten on his coat. He takes my temperature. Then I ask him to tell me a story. "All right," he says. "I shall tell you a story about a horse that could fly."

"Was he good?"

"*Good?* Why, he was so good, and so strong, and so great—he could be anything he wanted to be. A handsome prince. A soldier. A beggar. Anybody!"

"What was his name?"

"Vocapolos."

He begins the story. His voice fills the room like that of an actor speaking from a huge stage. In a moment I'm carried off to a mystical place. Through storm clouds and sunlight I see a snow-white horse with golden wings soar silently toward a distant summit. . . .

There were some things my father never told me. I often wondered why my grandparents separated for weeks at a time. It was always the same. One day they'd be together; the next day my grandfather would be packing his things in a battered suitcase and moving out of the apartment. If I asked my father for an explanation, he'd say, "Ask your mother."

"Grandpa's gone to Chicago," was the usual answer.

"Why?" I'd persist, pouting.

"To get a job."

How could she tell a six-year-old that an unhappy marriage was the cause of my grandfather's lengthy absences? But much later, when she felt I could handle it, the essential details came out.

Nothing had gone right for my grandfather back in Chicago's Greektown. One menial job followed another: waiter, janitor, night watchman—always a struggle and never a day that he could hold up his head and tell my grandmother: "Sophie, I've made it!"

When the great Depression hit in 1929, they came to live with us in Gary. And one day my grandfather finally spoke to my mother about the nagging doubt that plagued him throughout his life in America.

"Look at me," he said. "I'm nobody. A nothing."

"Pa, don't talk like that," she answered. "Your son loves you. We all love you. Isn't that enough?"

"What is *enough?* Maybe if I finished school in Athens, that would be enough. Maybe if I was a better son, a richer husband, a better father—that would be enough. But I'm none of these things. So it isn't enough."

Poor grandpa. He died when I was only six years old. My grandmother sat quietly at his bier for a long time. Before they closed the casket she leaned forward and gently touched his forehead. "Louie . . . Louie . . ." she whispered, "it's time to go home."

A few months later we moved from Adams Street, and I stepped from the shadows of infancy into a brighter light.

3. Distorted Mirrors

It's still there—that old house of mine. Once, it seemed gigantic and sturdy, as strong as any house ever built. I thought it would always be that way. But with the passage of time I've gained a new perspective. Now the house looks much smaller; five decades of use have spread a grimy coat over the brick walls outside. I painted those bricks a long time ago—a bright red. It's still red, although faded, like the odors and sounds that used to fill the rooms: the smell of lamb and peppers cooking in the white-tiled kitchen; the sound of piano scales in the parlor; Benny Goodman's clarinet coming from our Philco console radio; silent Sundays in my bedroom upstairs, where I would sit for hours with a vague sense of sadness; mom and dad talking and laughing downstairs; cold winter nights and winds that whistled me to sleep—and the high-pitched voices of Tony and Big Mesho and Chubby and Joe and Teddy and Paulie waking me on a bright spring morning. From such thoughts I leap back and, like sand through an hourglass, see the childhood pleasures and sorrows run out.

We lived at 724 Connecticut Street in Eastside Gary. On either side, from corner to corner, stood the modest, wood-frame houses of our neighbors, who were mostly Greek, Italian, Lebanese, Serbian, and Czech mill workers. Our house stood like a fortress; it was a two-story colonial with a wide, screened-in porch. Although it takes some doing to grow grass in the sandy soil of Gary, we were lucky: grass thrived in our backyard. So did a beautiful cherry tree that my father planted shortly after we moved in. I loved that cherry tree. It provided the fruit that went into my mother's pies on picnic Sundays.

In a neighborhood like ours, every house contained children of all sizes. So there were many young friends around to help me get through the bewilderment I felt after my grandfather's death. Tony Frangaskis was my best friend.

One day he came whooping down the street, holding something in his fist. "Look what I bought!"

A tiny green-backed turtle squatted on his palm, its eyes blinking sorrowfully in the sunlight.

"Wow! Where did you get it?"

"At Kresge's. Costs a nickel."

"Is it a boy or a girl?"

"I don't know. It's a turtle."

"I'm gonna get one."

Well, all that morning and late into the afternoon, no matter how much I coaxed and pleaded, no one in the family would give me a nickel. It was as if I had asked for a million dollars. Even tugging at mom's skirt didn't help. "I'm busy," she kept saying. "Go play with Tony."

Not yet. I dashed all the way to Kresge's at the corner of Broadway and Seventh Avenue. At the pet department I slipped my hand into the turtle tank while nobody was looking. I took two of them.

"Where did you get those turtles?" my mother demanded when I returned home.

"The man at Kresge's gave them to me."

"What man?"

My jaws wouldn't work. A crimson flush covered my face.

"Alex, did you take those turtles without paying for them?"

"Yes, mom. But only because . . ."

She pulled me up tight. "You take them back this very instant. *Do you hear me*? And tell the pet-department manager to telephone me. *Do you understand?*"

"Yes, mom . . ."

The turtles were returned to Kresge's as fast as a pair of seven-year-old legs could get them there. Shamefaced, I listened while the manager talked to my mother on the phone. "No, Mrs. Karras, I won't put your little boy in jail. I think he's learned his lesson. . . . Oh, that's quite all right. . . ." It was a harrowing experience, but well worth it. I never stole a turtle again.

The thing I remember most about those early times is that my brother Louie was the best athlete who ever played in the Sears Roebuck parking lot across the street from our house. Football was his passion. With a football under his arm and gravel kicking out from under his feet, Louie could be very dangerous. Maybe that's why so many motorists kept their cars parked elsewhere when he showed up for a game. Every kid stood in awe of my big brother. It was as though he had invisible powers—above and behind him. If he was in a good mood, the kids would relax and shine up to him. In a bad mood, they would scatter like birds. Even me. I was scared to death of Louie.

Art Rolfe, the football coach at Emerson High, took advantage of Louie's toughness. Rolfe recruited him as a junior varsity player, then switched him over to varsity. In his freshman year Louie outmuscled every opponent in the conference.

The next summer he worked in the steel mill. The country was in the middle of World War II, and Gary needed all the skilled and unskilled labor it could get in order to feed guns and fuel to our armed forces. Although I was too young to understand what the war was all about, I vaguely recall the talk about Pearl Harbor, and the sight of the Stars and Stripes flapping in almost every front yard on our block.

Then, a terrible shock! It told me more about the meaning of war than all the patriotic-sounding speeches or brass-band parades that took place in Gary during the early and mid-forties.

Jimmy Swan, who lived a few houses away, was a great football player at Emerson High. Shortly after graduation he enlisted in the navy. Before going overseas he stopped by to see my parents. How clearly I remember the day. He stood on our front porch, sun-warmed and smiling in his navy blues, shaking my father's hand while I shyly looked on.

Some weeks later I noticed a gold star in the window of Jimmy's house. I asked my father what it meant. "God wants Jimmy in heaven, where there are no wars," he said.

That night, and for many nights after, the mystery of life and death gripped me in a stranglehold of fear. I had been prepared for my grandfather's death. In his last days he looked thin and shrunken, like a wax doll. But Jimmy Swan was young and powerful. If he could die, then all of us would die. Dad. Mom. All my brothers. And sister. Everybody!

"For what reason?" I asked the darkness around me. A hollow silence answered.

The reassuring pleasures soon returned, with boundless opportunities to find all sorts of new trouble to get into.

For instance, watching Louie play, I learned to run

fast enough and long enough to avoid being caught by the police.

At seventeen Louie had grown to full size: six-four, and 250 pounds. He was the toughest, roughest teenager in Eastside Gary. People backed into doorways when they saw him coming around the corner. So Tony and I hung around with Teddy and his friends. On autumn Saturdays we'd go over to Gleason Field to watch Louie play. It cost a quarter to get in. We never had the price of admission, so we'd take up a collection, put together twenty-five cents, and I'd stick it in my pocket. I was always the decoy, the rabbit who would lead the hares over a tall, barbed-wire fence at the back of the stadium.

First, the gang would form a human pyramid, boost me to the top of the fence, and I'd drop down all cut and bleeding from the barbs. Once inside, scat! But not before I made sure the cops had spotted me. That was the trick. Give the scent, and *go!* I ran with all my might, dodging and weaving across the field until everyone got over the fence. I loved it, the excitement, the crowd roaring and cheering as I scooted left and right, always just beyond the reach of the fastest cop. Eventually, they caught up to me. But I had the quarter, and they let me find a seat in the stands. The rest of the gang was already there—free of charge.

During that period Teddy began to dominate me in a more direct way than Louie ever did. There were moments when Teddy made my life miserable. Especially in the parking lot, where his quick temper flared every time I scored a winning touchdown against his team, did well in a basketball game, or managed to get a hit off him in a stickball game. I'm sure he acted that way without realizing how or why sibling rivalries start. Anyway, Teddy *never* stopped trying to emulate Louie. To this end he'd drive himself—to the brink if necessary—in order to gain the same kind of respect that Louie had commanded from all the kids in the neighborhood. Whenever I did something that topped Teddy's best efforts, he'd go absolutely wild. On more than one occasion Louie had to step in to make sure Teddy didn't kill me.

As hard as Louie and Teddy were, my brother Nick turned out to be the complete opposite. Nick was the sad-eyed dreamer of the Karras boys. The world of music mingled in his mind with thoughts that could not be penetrated by the rest of us. For Nick, in his younger years, displayed an unrelenting coolness to the physical activities of his brothers. He rarely took part in the games that went on in the parking lot or over at Eastside Park. When he did get involved, Louie or Teddy would usually razz him for being inept or awkward. Well, if Nick was born for anything, it wasn't to be an athlete. Fate took care of that during infancy, when a near-fatal bout with double pneumonia more than likely altered his natural growth. His slight frame, delicate bone structure, and lack of physical power stuck out incongruously in the Karras strain. So Nick turned to music; he took violin lessons. At about the same time, my sister, Helene, began her lifelong interest in the piano.

Christmas 1945. The Karras family is gathered in the parlor, opening presents, exchanging Yuletide greetings, happy, grateful, pleased to be with one another. Now it's time for Nick to play a violin solo: "Ave Maria." The music floats about my ears. Then something peculiar happens. My heaviest doubts disappear. I want to reach out, to say without hesitation: "I know you, Nick. I'm glad you're my brother."

It goes no further. A mounting uneasiness causes me

to yawn. Within minutes I close my eyes and drift off into a puzzled sleep.

I have reached an age that brings about sudden bursts of farseeing imagination. I spend hours on end gazing at distorted mirrors that open into a wonderland of adventure—where virtue always triumphs over evil. Through the glimmering maze I begin to see my father as one would see a living god: possessed with all the virtues, capable of the most heroic deeds, and having the qualities of love and compassion beyond the grasp of ordinary mortals. In a word, I *worship* him.

He's an imposing man, with a healthy crop of curly black hair, deep brown eyes, and a warm, outgoing smile. He nonetheless wears faded, wrinkled suits. They hang on him like a sack. His thin ties, flecked with sauce stains, never quite make it to the top button of his shirt collar. As far as fashion goes, my father dresses like Wallace Beery—out of an old *Min and Bill* movie.

What a pity his suits are lifeless things. Otherwise they would tell stories about Doctor George, who can stuff countless items into every pocket: pens, pencils, thermometers, note pads, prescription blanks, rubber bands, gambling slips, cigars, hard candy, a bulging wallet—so much trivia mixed with so many jottings about the people who depend on him during their troubled hours of illness.

Dad's a man of learning. He admires the finer things, such as music, art, and philosophy. In the privacy of his home he listens to Caruso and Toscanini on the phonograph, and reads deeply into Plato and Thoreau. But in the raw, smoky neighborhood outside, he sees little that reminds him of a superior civilization. No great libraries, magnificent museums, or splendid concert halls grace the streets of Gary.

What exists, for all of us, are the realities of drab
wooden houses, somber schools and churches, neon-lit
pool rooms, garish bars, and trolley cars that clatter
past the Wabash Railroad tracks to the giant mills,
where waves of orange-blue flame spew into the sky
and suck the breath out of the steelworkers. This is
what my father sees, and learns to live with.

The desire to know him better grew as I grew. In
the summer, when school let out, I would walk with
him from our house to his office on Broadway; past
the wooden row houses with front lawns that were
more sand than grass. In the alley, dark and sinister
even in the daylight, we occasionally saw a big rat.

"Tffff . . ." we spat. Then, at the same time: "Not
in *our* family."

Amen.

My father's office was two rooms atop the Grand
movie theater. It would take me forever to climb the
dimly lit, long, narrow staircase. Then, beyond the
landing, door after door of pebbled glass, with black
lettering: BAILBONDSMAN, DENTIST, ATTORNEY-AT-LAW,
And, finally, GEORGE KARRAS, M.D.

A cardboard clock hung by a string on the
doorknob: DOCTOR OUT. WILL BE BACK AT—— Every
morning he removed it, opened his office, and saw his
patients. The worst thing about his office was the reception area. A cold place. Horrible furniture; sticks
of wood supporting cracked leather cushions. And
ashtrays everywhere, filled with crushed cigarettes
and cigar butts. A catastrophe. His patients sat around
and waited to be called. Mill workers, mostly. They
sat around in rumpled clothes, with melancholy eyes,
fingernails crusted black, and honest dirt on their
faces. They sat and waited to be called into the examining room.

There was no receptionist; just my father, who'd

stick his head out every few minutes, point to some-one, and say, "Next."

He never said, "You're next, Mr. Brown." Or, "In here, Mr. Green." Never. Maybe it took too long. Maybe he didn't remember their names. I don't know. I think he wanted to get them into his office fast so that he could get them well fast.

I remember a framed document that hung on the wall behind his office desk.

"What is that?" I asked one day, pointing to it.

"You really want to know? All right—come, sit down. I'll tell you."

He sat me on a swivel chair, cupped my face in his hands, and looked intently into my eyes. "There's nothing to be compared with it. It's the Oath of Hippocrates."

"What?"

"Hippocrates. He was a doctor."

"Like you?"

"In a way, yes. He was Greek. He lived hundreds of years ago. And those words up on the wall were written even before Jesus was born."

"What does it say?"

Still looking into my eyes, he began: "I swear by Apollo, the physician, and Asclepius and Health and Panacea, and all the gods and goddesses . . ."

"I don't understand that."

He laughed. "That's okay. Neither did I. Not for a long time." He walked over to the wall. "These are rules, Alex. Simple rules that I must follow—just like Hippocrates did—if I expect to be a good doctor. They tell me to belive in facts, not in magic or su-perstition. They tell me to practice medicine with kindness to those who are suffering. And whatever house I enter . . . not to go in unless my heart is pure."

A day or so later I looked up Hippocrates in the school library. His picture was in the encyclopedia. He had a pudgy nose, just like my father's.

4. My Gang

Like my older brothers and sister before me, and
Paulie afterward, I attended Gary Emerson grammar
school. It also served as our high school.

Built in the early twenties, Emerson was the first
work-play-study school in the nation. USS subsidized
most of the construction, for a good reason: to show
the semiliterate mill workers that their kids would re-
ceive—through the blessings of God and USS—a decent education and a chance to go on to college. I saw
none of those visions as a child. Only the sight of a
shabby, three-story elementary school, with creaky
wooden floors, creaky desks branded by hundreds of
penknives belonging to former students, and creaky
old teachers who always seemed to be looking at their
watches. Looking to go home. Like me.

What is it about a child's sense of age? I mean, tired
old age, whether it be worn-out buildings or worn-
out people. I only know that Emerson and its teachers
depressed me. Each day I felt as if I had walked into a
prison. I imagined doors clanging shut. I saw myself
bearded, in rags, scraping the dungeon walls with a tin
cup to keep track of the days. Bleak, empty days ex-
tending into nothingness. A forlorn existence in a
school that pulsed with anger. And always the teachers. Old and bitter. Hating the school almost as much
as I did. From the third grade up I was taught to read
and write by wrinkled fossils. They padded around

with rancid breath and hot tempers. If a student committed the slightest offense, swift punishment followed. If he resisted, the results were very painful.

One day I decided to make myself heard. I was sitting in the back row of the arithmetic class. Minnie Talbot, a ninety-eight-year-old venerable weighing about eighty pounds, with orthopedic shoes laced up to her ankles, stood at the blackboard, pointing at multiplication examples with a long metal ruler. I couldn't hear a word she said.

I jump up. "Miss Talbot, could I ask you a question?"

Bony fingers twist around the ruler. "What was that, young man?"

She marches up the aisle to my desk. "It is *may* I . . . not *could* I, young man."

The ruler slams against the side of my head. Whap! Pain races into my neck and shoulders. It takes my breath away. I sit down, trembling.

And from that moment on, I never ask another question at Emerson grade school.

One great thing about school, though. It always recessed. Once the final bell rang, I flew out to the street and straight to Eastside Park, which rose out of the ground like an oasis.

The park was a marvelous place. It had everything: space, grass, swings, teeter-totters, a basketball court, a shallow swimming pool, and a bathhouse. There I first came to know other kids besides Tony Frangaskis and my brothers. In the evenings, we turned the bathhouse into a meeting room. We planned ball games, fell into disputes, levied fines, and, with a great deal of imagination, conducted ourselves as though we were in a vast Hall of Justice.

Tony Autominelli ruled the gang. He was the oldest, which automatically made him the wisest, most superior leader of the Eastside. At fifteen he rode a motorcycle, drove a power boat all over Lake Michigan, organized beer parties in the park, and played high-roll dice games in the darkest cellars and spookiest alleys. Tony knew how to make a buck.

My brother Teddy was our best player. And our bravest. He led all the charges when we crushed the Westside kids in football games. He knocked down their passes and tackled the toughest ball carriers. In baseball, he swung his bat like Phil Cavarretta blasting a homer into the seats at Wrigley Field. On a basketball court, his body blocks made cowards out of the most courageous opponents. We looked to Teddy as our warrior chief.

Chubby Tansky got his name because he had fat cheeks and a fatter belly. Next to Teddy, he was our best tackle.

Donny Coleman wore black hornrimmed glasses that framed the most threatening pair of eyes I ever looked into. They gave me the creeps. Another peculiar thing about Donny—he began to smoke cigarettes at the age of ten. Like a chimney. He always carried a pack with him, rolled up in the sleeve of his T-shirt. I'm sure he did this to look impressive. When he smoked, he had a habit of pulling in his neck, and his eyes danced back and forth as though any second a bomb would fall and blow him to bits. Donny was totally insecure.

Joe Cash, on the other hand, had a very trusting nature. He never got into fights or said anything out of the way to anyone. A skinny, pimply-faced boy, he had come up from the South with his parents and twin sister. His parents were gaunt, tired people who worked in the mill and hungered for the smell of flowers and sun and fresh earth—the country things of their past. But Mrs. Cash couldn't keep a plant alive in her house. The place was as dark as a tomb.

Tony Frangaskis oozed cheerfulness. I guess he was the happiest kid I ever knew. Still, another side of him came through whenever he spoke about his mother. She had a rheumatic heart and was under my father's care.

"Someday I'm going to be an actor," he'd say. "When I'm rich, I'll take my mother away . . . to the mountains . . . so she can breathe. The air stinks around here."

As long as I can remember, Tony wanted to be an actor. He even had a name picked out for himself. Tony Frank. "That's a real name," he'd say. "It sure beats Tony Frangaskis. What kind of a name is that? Nobody'd remember it. Nobody."

So I always called him Tony Frank. And hoped he'd become a big movie star. And get rich. And take his mother far away from Gary, Indiana. I hoped he'd take me along, too.

My gang. And more: my brother Paulie, Don and Gene Onerfrey, Don Freeman (we had lots of Dons), Nick Malham, Guy Vitucci, and Mike Nahod—everyone called him Big Mesho. I hear them now. I see them on a September day in Gary; I am eleven years old.

We're shooting baskets under a brilliant sun. The air is warm. Mothers wheel their baby carriages through the park. Grandfathers sit on benches and gossip about the atomic bomb and Social Security and the National League pennant race. A perfect day. We're happy.

Suddenly Chubby yells, "Here comes Big Mesho." He approaches, with a wide grin on his face. A girl of twelve or so holds his hand; she's a freckle-faced, pug-nosed kid with a hint of bosom showing beneath her sweater.

"Who's that?" Donny Coleman asks, pulling his neck in and taking a drag on his cigarette. Big Mesho introduces the girl. "This is Alice. She's from the Westside."

Donny glares at her suspiciously, then spits tobacco bits out of his mouth. "We don't play with girls," he grumbles.

Big Mesho ignores the remark. He puts his arm around Alice, and she buttons her sweater.

"Ah . . . let's shoot baskets," says Donny, starting a dribble to the hoop.

Big Mesho shrugs. "I'm walking Alice home. See you later."

I know he has been hurt by Donny's peevish attitude toward Alice. Everyone knows it. But we don't say anything. And Big Mesho walks out of the park with Alice. We go back to shooting baskets. A while later, Donny says:

"I bet Big Mesho is giving it to her."

"Giving her what?"

"You know. What are you . . . stupid? A quarter says he's screwing her."

"Huh?"

"Screwing her. Don't you—ah—you must be stupid."

"Yeah? Well, you're a liar. Big Mesho wouldn't do a thing like that. He's not old enough."

Later that night I creep into my house and try to forget Donny Coleman's words. Instead, I fall asleep with a prayer on my lips: "Please, God, the next time Donny bets on anything—let me have a quarter."

Connecticut Street. Where every front door was open. Who would ever think of breaking into our homes? Who would dare rob us? Or rape our women? Or murder our fathers? Not in our neighborhood! Other things concerned us. The children played and went to school. The fathers worked. The mothers cooked. The cooking smells came at us in waves, fanning our noses as we walked past the open doors. There were old-world dishes like lasagna and pilaf, sauerbraten and goulash, chicken legs in wine sauce and fish heads dipped in garlic. And new-world dishes like Mexican chili con carne, Canadian meat pies, and Cajun country cooking. But nothing American. Campbell's Soup never reached our table. Mom made her own soups that shimmered and swelled with fat chunks of potatoes and carrots and red meat. She took special pride in serving pilaf, which is rice and chicken livers baked in a casserole with tomatoes, celery, paprika, chopped nuts, and grated cheese. I loved pilaf, and couldn't imagine anyone who didn't.

One spring day I met Joe Cash on the street. He was starving. He didn't exactly say so. It was the way he acted.

"My sister and parents won't be home until after dark," Joe said, rubbing his skinny belly.

"Come over to my house. We're having pilaf."

Joe had three helpings, then went home with his belly sticking out. The next day he missed school. My father looked in on him and said Joe had a gigantic stomachache, probably caused by a radical change in his diet. "He's been on pork and beans so long, they should've named him Heinz Fifty-seven."

It's autumn. I'm eating lunch at home with my brothers. Nick has a bandage plastered over his broken nose. Louie keeps looking at it as though the injury doesn't deserve his pity. We eat quietly, with gazes shifting from face to face. When the meal ends, Nick goes to his room and slams the door.

"What's wrong with him?" Teddy asks my mother. "His nose will heal."

"It's his heart I'm worrying about," she answers. "That takes a little longer."

Food for thought. A whole life changes because of a chance accident. Or a series of accidents, when minds and bodies thoughtlessly hurl themselves at each other—day after day—until someone gets hurt; until something inborn is damaged beyond repair. What is the sense to it?

In his senior year at Gary Emerson, Louie received football-scholarship offers from every section of the country. At eighteen he was tall enough, strong enough, and popular enough to be anything he wanted. Louie didn't hesitate. He chose football, and went away to Purdue University to become an All-America tackle.

Nick didn't go to college. He quit Emerson during his junior year. I think a lot of other things ended for him while he was still a freshman and realized he wasn't good enough to play football in the same league with Louie. After Nick had his nose busted, he didn't seem to care very much about anything.

In his room, sitting on the bed, Nick gingerly touches his bandaged nose.

"Does it hurt?" I ask timidly.

"Of course it hurts."

"Louie said you were bleeding a lot. What happened?"

"Nothing happened. I just got hit. We were blocking. Somebody hit me. First day of freshman practice and I get my nose broken. Ain't that something?"

"Yeah. Did you cry?"

"What, me cry? With Louie around? Are you crazy?"

"Louie said you looked scared."

"Louie can take a jump for himself. What does he know? I never should've . . ." Nick gets up from the bed, agitated. "Leave me alone, will you? Go downstairs."

I close the door and go downstairs. Louie's doing his homework at the dining-room table. I want to talk to him but don't know what to say. So I go out into the streets, galloping off to wherever the wind takes me, as long as it leads away from sadness.

In the streets of Gary I concentrate on happy thoughts. The streets sing my name and open a path to Eastside Park, and the pool room, and the movie houses, and dad's office. The streets beckon and I run, hypnotized, to all the good times that are just around the corner.

I see Sam the Banana on the street. Look at that nose! I see it from a block away. A giant of a nose—criss-crossed with bulging veins. It's stuck on his round, blue-red face like a monstrous growth.

"Hey, Sam. Where are you going?"

"To see the boss. Come, we go. Okay?"

We walk down Broadway to dad's office—with me out front because Sam the Banana moves like a snail.

His real name is Sam Bellos. He's a baggy-pants drifter; a middle-aged, barely educated Greek who looks older than a mountain and has a body that's been ravished by every ailment in the book. His main problem is diabetes. He manufactures sugar like Jack Frost. On his bad days, Sam's face goes to technicolor and he gets very dizzy. When people see him like that they shake their heads and think he's been hitting the bottle. But Sam never drinks. If he did, it would kill him. Fortunately, dad keeps him alive. He sticks needles into Sam's tormented body and presses money into his pocket. He pays all his hospital, hotel, and restaurant bills. And Sam responds with unswerving loyalty. He's always doing something for my father. Running down to the pharmacy to get a few prescriptions filled, or driving a patient to Methodist Hospital, or cleaning out the furnace at our house.

Poor fellow. He has no family. He lives in a little room at the Y. Every day he struggles back and forth across Gary until his strength gives out. Then he beds down for the night, snoring through his incredible nose—all alone with his diabetes and his long-lost dreams.

Anyway, we make it up the stairs. Now we're in the waiting room. My father comes out, a stethoscope still in his ears.

"What's for today, boss?" Sam asks.

"Never mind today. Did you take your medicine last night?"

"Sure, boss." Never Dr. Karras. Or doc. Always boss.

My father sighs, then whispers something. But I can make it out:

"Lay a deuce on Lucky Lady in the third at Arlington."

"Okay, boss."

"Next!" A patient goes into the examining room. Now dad looks at me. "What is it?"

"I want to talk to you about Nick. You know . . . his accident."

"Don't worry. Nick will be all right. It's a simple fracture." He brings me close against his side. "Listen, Alex, I'm a little busy right now. See you at home." He hands me a dime. "Clean out the ashtrays, then take in a movie. Gary Cooper's playing downstairs."

I forget about Nick. I empty a pile of cigarette butts and squashed cigars, then go down to the street. But I don't see the movie. I rush over to the pool room to be with my gang. In the pool room I can shoot a game of eight-ball, smoke, cuss, sit around with the grownups, and watch Sam the Banana place a two-dollar bet for my father on Lucky Lady.

Chubby Tansky and I square off in a game. The gang's making side bets, nickels and dimes riding on each shot. Chubby clears all but one of his even-numbered balls, then sets up the six-ball with the aid of a bridge. "Side pocket. . . . Damn! Too much English. I'll get it next shot."

No way. I pick off the odd-numbered balls like a marine sharpshooter. One more to go—a black crescent lurking behind Chubby's six-ball. Casually, I wave the cue stick toward the far right pocket. "In there . . ."

"A dime says he don't make it," says Donny Coleman.

Tony Frank slaps a coin on the table. "Covered."

Whammo! The eight-ball hits the far cushion, whizzes back, drops into the far right pocket. "Game!" I call out ecstatically.

Donny's face turns purple. "I'll rip you apart! I'll break your ass! You pointed left!" He moves to the cue rack—a frenzied pulling at one of the sticks.

"Are you nuts?" Tony Frank yells. He grabs Donny around the neck, at the same time locking his arm in a judo hold. "Leave Al alone. Cut it out!"

"Okay—let go! You're busting my arm!"

A ripple of uneasy laughter. We split up and go home. I feel humiliated. It's my fight, not Tony's. But I've chickened out. Why? I can crush Donny like a gnat. Wipe the floor with him. Destroy him with one punch. But the moment's passed. I walk home baffled, expecting trouble from Donny at any time.

It happens the next morning, a few doors from my house. Donny comes at me with his arms churning, spitting curses, swooping down from nowhere like a bird of prey. In an instant we're rolling on the sidewalk. The asphalt scrapes away skin and burns a strawberry into my cheek. "You dirty rat!" he shouts. "You pointed left . . . *left!*"

A car turns the corner. From the pavement, I see Louie behind the wheel, coming home from a jog on the beach. Then I hear him bellowing: "Sonofabitch ... get the hell off!"

Donny's removed from my back like a stone hoisted up by a derrick. I scramble to my feet. Louie releases his grip and Donny drops to the sidewalk in a lump.

"You touch my brother again," says Louie, "I'll put you in the hospital." For emphasis, he pulls Donny erect, kicks his behind, and sends him howling down the street like he's on fire.

My shirt is ripped, and there's a slight bruise under my eye. "Better wash up," Louie says. "And change your clothes before mom sees you. Goddamn, Al, you gotta learn how to protect yourself. You're bigger than him."

5. Everybody Needs My Father

Whatever success my father had as a doctor, there were bad moments, too. Moments of total depression. I mention this because at the age of thirteen I had limited understanding of the personal struggles, the sense of stress, the powerful forces that frustrated him day after day. Sure, I could see signs. They were on his face. In his eyes. In the way he got up from a chair when the phone rang, in the way he laughed, and ate, and listened to music. In so many ways. Mostly, I saw that he didn't want to break away from his family and go out into the night on house calls, or go over to Methodist Hospital to operate on one of his patients, then come home with tears in his eyes when something went wrong. I saw all that. But I wasn't old enough to know that the attainment of complete happiness can never be reached by any man, even if he happens to be someone like my father.

A spring morning in 1948. My father has returned from a house call. I stand by the bathroom door and see the muscles along his shoulders and arms tighten as he leans over the sink. There's so much strength in him, and yet he seems very tired, falling-down tired. Now he reaches for a towel, and catches me staring at him. Feeling strangely uneasy, I start off for my room.

"Aren't you going to say good night?"

I turn and come back. In the glare of the bathroom
light, his face is stone gray, his eyes dull. They're
filled with resignation.

"Good night," I mumble. A moment later the
phone rings. He goes downstairs to answer it. From
the top steps I hear his voice. It rises from a hoarse
rumble to a thickening roar. It rips through the house
like a thunderstorm.

"What the hell . . . No, no, no . . . Goddamnit,
Sam, just stay there! Yes . . . I'll be over in twenty
minutes with the insulin. . . . Listen to me, you stupid dumb Greek! Just stay there and wait!"

He hangs up. And bellows at the top of his lungs:
"*Stupid! Stupid! Stupid!*"

Late spring. I'm with dad and Teddy on the bank
of the Kankakee River in Illinois, our fishing poles
held loosely over the water. Everything's so peaceful
—puffy clouds, the smell of damp earth, birds chirping.
We have the whole day to enjoy.

"The pole's moving. Look!"

Dad jumps up, takes a firm grip, and starts to reel in
his line. The water breaks. An olive-bellied fish with a
milk-white fin struggles to get loose. It fails. And
Teddy's yelling, "Wow! Look at that! It's a
monster!"

Night is coming on as we cross into Indiana in dad's
battered Dodge. The adventure is behind us. "Wait'll
your mother sees our fish," he says. The moment
freezes in my mind. Maybe because we've never been
together like this.

Early summer. I've come home from school with
Tony Frank. A new Chrysler is parked at the curb. A
shiny blue thing, fully equipped, with white wheels
and chrome hubcaps—and my father is sitting behind

the wheel, a proud grin on his face. "Get in," he says to us. "Let's take a ride around the block."

How many automobiles has he owned before this? Three? Maybe four? All of them secondhand—something to move around in and nothing to brag about. But *this* car is a brilliant blur under the summer sun. Tony and I sink down on the soft, fresh-smelling upholstery. The car starts to roll down Connecticut Street, purring, the sound a beautiful rhythm in my ears. And suddenly I realize how hard it must have been for my father to save up for the Chrysler. A picture forms in my mind—the memory of how once at the supper table my mother had bitterly complained that his patients were not paying their bills. "We have to eat, too," she said. "Why can't you collect from them? They take advantage." She wept. "Well," my father said, "they'd pay if they could. Anyway, we have enough money to get by. Let's just get the job done." And my mother said, "In that case, Dr. Karras, you'll have to live forever."

The ride is over. "Have fun," says dad, and drives off to see one of his patients at Methodist Hospital. I stand on the sidewalk in silence for several minutes, then turn to Tony and say, "Let's go over to the park. C'mon, we'll have some fun."

August. The brightest of days. We pile into dad's Chrysler—Teddy and Paulie and Tony Frank and dad and me—and go to Michigan City for a picnic on the beach. In the trunk of the car we have a large bag of charcoal, a case of Coca-Cola, and plenty of hot dogs and buns. What a day it's going to be!

"Hurry up, dad, we're hungry," Teddy says on the beach. We've been standing around the barbecue pit, waiting for my father to place hot dogs over the coals. They've been glowing for an hour.

"They're not ready," he replies. "They have to flame."

"No," says Tony Frank. "When the charcoals are red, they're hot enough to cook on."

"Are you sure?"

"Yeah, Doctor George. My folks took me here one time. I saw how it's done."

"Hmmm."

The sun dips. The wind, cooler now, rustles on the sand like a soft whisper. A few people sit quietly along the beach, their hunched bodies nothing more than scattered boulders in a vast desert.

"Had enough to eat?" dad asks. The kids nod. He gets up shakily from the sand, his pants rolled up over the ankles. They're swollen tightly, swollen like I've never seen them before. We walk to our car, with me and Teddy behind dad. He stops every once in a while to catch his breath.

September comes. I'm having eye problems. Before school starts, mom takes me to the optometrist and he fits me with a pair of glasses.

The gang is playing football in the parking lot. Dad's watching from his bedroom on the second floor, his face a white dot in the window.

Teddy is our quarterback. I'm the center. Tony Autominelli, who's been playing at end, has just fallen on the gravel and sprained his wrist. He goes home. We need a substitute.

"Get in here and play center," Teddy tells my brother Paulie. In another year or two he'll be big enough to join the gang in all our games. But now it's an emergency, so he races over, thrilled, his grin spreading like a sunrise.

"Okay, Al," Teddy says in the huddle. "You're the receiver. Here's the play. Go down about twenty-five yards, then take a left at the Studebaker. And don't fuck up."

"I won't."

"If you do, I'll kill ya."

The gravel flies. The ball comes over my head. A perfect spiral. Reaching out—stretching, straining, in one last aching lunge I guide the ball into my hand, bounce off a Hudson convertible, and sprint another five yards for a touchdown. It's the greatest catch anybody's ever made in the old Sears Roebuck parking lot!

I look across the street and see dad. He hasn't missed a thing. "Hold it, I'll be right back," I say to Teddy, then run across the street, into the house, up the stairs, and throw open the door to my father's bedroom.

"Did you see it?"

"Yes. You know, you're terrific. Someday you'll be a better athlete than Louie or Teddy."

I don't say anything. I just stand there, staring dumbly, with my mouth open and my heart beating a mile a minute.

I go over to his chair. He's lost a lot of weight. Only his ankles are heavy. God, they look like balloons. Why doesn't the swelling go down? Why can't he get well? Why can't he go back to work? His patients need him. Everybody needs him. Christ in heaven, please make my father well.

"Can I get you anything, dad?"

"No. I'm fine."

"Well . . . okay. And thanks. Thanks a lot."

A scream. Mom is screaming. Helene comes half-way down the stairs, her eyes filled with terror. "Come up, come up! Hurry!"

I look through a gauze of light and see frozen figures standing on either side of my father's bed. His feet are uncovered. They're chalk white, rigid. Then they relax.

Run, Alex, run. Get out of the house. Go to school. Run! Run away from sorrow. Run away from grief. And whatever you do, don't cry. Goddamnit, don't you ever ever ever cry!

6. Dear Miss Potts

There were seven high schools in Gary back in 1949. Emerson had the best football team and, in my opinion, the best coach in the state of Indiana. His name was Art Rolfe. He didn't lie, double-talk, or play politics with anyone. Long after he retired from the school system, I had an opportunity to say those things about him at a testimonial dinner given in his honor. I think of him now. And I see Teddy—then a junior All-State guard—as he walks up to me on our first day of junior varsity practice.

"What are you doing here?"

"Trying to make the freshman team . . . that's what."

"Well, Coach Rolfe wants you to work out with the varsity."

The varsity team is loaded with Gargantuans. They walk around with hair under their arms. Some even have beards.

"Do you think I can cut it with those guys?"

"You're a Karras, aren't you?" Teddy snarls.

Rolfe was in his early fifties, then, a bald-headed Adonis with arms of steel, concrete shoulders, and dynamite legs. I'll never forget those legs. On chilly, blustery mornings he'd come out to practice in a pair of gold and blue shorts (our team colors) to show them off. If a female teacher happened to be around, so much the better. He'd hitch up the shorts, smooth his hands up and down his thighs, then start trotting around the field like a stallion. Old Art was quite a ladies' man. A widower with two grown sons, he figured he had every right to go out with anyone he wanted.

Coach Rolfe's basic approach to the game was formed on a simple but sound principle: "You can always run with the ball," he'd say, "but it don't mean a thing if nobody's blocking or tackling in there."

He invariably ended his sentences with "in there." He'd say things like, "You gotta be tough *in there* . . . Stop fucking around *in there* . . . That's a nice tackle *in there* . . ." and so on. One time he caught a student who didn't belong in the locker room. "What are you doing in here *in there*?" he hollered. Honest.

Anyway, Rolfe promoted me to the varsity squad one week after I enrolled as a freshman. He sent me in as a scrub tackle, on the same side of the line as Teddy. A few days later the starting tackle broke his leg. Right after that the kid who moved up to the first string broke his shoulder. So I became the number-one tackle.

We opened against Muncie Central High. A heavyweight team. Real giants. They could inflict terrible punishment at any moment. So I imagined telling the Muncie linemen, "Listen, you guys, Teddy Karras is my brother. You better not beat me up too bad."

We played under the lights on a night so cold that most of us were frozen stiff before the opening kickoff. While we huddled for instructions, Muncie took the field and began to whoop it up. They circled us like Indians around a wagon train. Their faces were mean, and ugly as sin. One of them got real close. *"How-dee-dooooo! We're gonna' knock your dicks off!"* I looked for the nearest exit. But Teddy stopped me with a withering stare. I went back to the huddle knowing it was going to be the very last game of my life.

It almost turned out that way. Muncie slaughtered us. And a killer guard hit me so hard on one play I reverberated like the gong in a J. Arthur Rank movie. The trainer had to revive me with smelling salts. Late that night my mother stuck me in bed. "Stay there until I tell you to get out. You've had a concussion." I also had a legitimate excuse to stay away from football for a few days. Even Teddy would have to admit it couldn't be helped.

I came back the following week, playing hard and well. At season's end, we won the city championship and the sectionals, and went down to play South Bend Central for the state title. Something like twenty-five thousand people filled the stadium, the largest crowd I'd ever seen. What a thrill! Under that kind of pressure, Emerson played an inspired game.

We lost. Just barely.

All the same, it was a worthwhile experience. Not so much in what I learned as a football player, but in the fact that I began to develop a keen interest in the reactions as well as the character of people who attend sporting events. Aside from the drunks, one fellow in particular comes to mind.

During our three days of practice in South Bend, Central's team doctor would often stop by to chat with the Emerson players. He was amiable, sincere, attentive. He conducted himself like the nicest individual God ever put on earth. But once the game started, there was a definite change in his personality.

"Kill those Gary bastards!" he swore. "Tear 'em to pieces! Rip their goddamn hearts out!"

In the spring I played baseball, hitting home runs against Hammond, East Chicago, Muncie Central, and a few other schools outside Gary. I couldn't have been happier. I was on my own, no longer in competition with Louie and Teddy. They leaned steadily toward football. Out of their shadow, I concentrated on baseball and hoped that someday, in the not too distant future, I would be in the starting lineup of a major league club.

One morning Tony Frank and I took a bus to Chicago to watch the Brooklyn Dodgers play the Cubs at Wrigley Field. I was a Dodger fan ever since Jackie Robinson joined the team in 1947.

Jackie Robinson. I knew where he came from and how he came. I could relate to that. I could identify with him. Not in his blackness, but in the way he withstood all those terrible things. The insults. The curses. The threats. The man stood up. He saw his way through. I admired him for that.

"There he is!" I yelled when Jackie Robinson and his teammates ran out for infield practice. I saw his uniform—the number 42 on his gray flannel shirt. I saw his sureness, the power in his body, the quick gliding flash of feet and hands, the eyes black with want. I saw him. He was far away, yet so close.

Someday, I thought, I would catch for the Dodgers. And Jackie Robinson would be guarding third base. Or left field. We'd be teammates. I could see it.

Every pitch moved in like a twisting blur during my sophomore year at Emerson. Then my eyes got worse. I couldn't see the curve anymore. So I changed my glasses. It didn't help. I just couldn't see the curve. But, bad eyes or no, I still had a great arm. I made the city All-Star team that year. A St. Louis Browns scout came to Gary with the idea of signing me to a contract.

"Mr. Veeck thinks you can make our ball club," he said. Bill Veeck owned the Browns. He had seen me play. He liked the way I swung the bat. But he didn't know about my eyes. Now his bird dog was at my house, talking about my future, talking about life in the "bigs," talking about backstops like Roy Campanella, Andy Seminick, Yogi Berra, and Sherm Lollar. He kept getting back to Lollar, who caught for the Browns.

"You never know. You may be taking over Sherm's job in five or six years. That is, if he's with us by then. You never know . . ."

I said, "Sir, I'd love to play for Mr. Veeck. But I can't."

"How's that, kid?"

"My eyes. I can't see the curve."

He went away. And I sat out on the front porch, watching him go, all the while feeling scared and lonely and wishing I had never been born.

The end of the spring term. Emerson's Spice and Variety Club put on a musical—*South Pacific*. I played one of the sailors. The biggest laugh came when I stuck my stomach way out—tight as a drum—while we were singing "There Is Nothing Like a Dame." Everyone in the audience howled. But only Miss Potts knew how much I wanted to be appreciated as an actor, and not just a jock on stage trying to be funny.

She was my English teacher, a radiant Irish lady who had come all the way from Dublin to teach at Gary Emerson until summer recess. She had rust-colored hair and green eyes and a glowing smile. Her body was graceful and full of curves. Sometimes, while sitting in her class, I would feel a swell of emotion for Miss Potts. Then, in shame, I forced myself to think of other things.

I was supposed to be tough, not get involved with the opposite sex. Besides, the coaches kept a steady eye on the athletes just to make sure. "Save your strength for the game," they'd say if we were caught

looking sideways at the cheerleaders, or at any of the
Emerson girls, for that matter. They'd use that line all
the time. Even before our school dances, which were
always a big bore and—worse yet—very undemocratic.
I mean, the dances were segregated! Every dance
would start out with the girls lined up on one side,
boys on the other, and end that way—with the boys
going home completely frustrated. I gave up going to
the dances. And didn't have much contact with girls
after that on any level. Then I met Miss Potts.

At first there was no big thing about it. There were
smiles exchanged. In the classroom. In the hall. On the
staircase. Little incidents. Once, when I stayed after
class to erase the blackboard, she called me a wonderful person. It was as if she had lifted me high above
the hundreds of Emerson students and said—"Look
here, this is a *somebody*." Just then, I had a tremendous urge to kiss her. But I wouldn't dare.

One day after class we got into close quarters at the
blackboard. Close enough that I could smell the
fragrance of her body. I had an erection. Miss Potts
brushed against it. Forgetting everything except what
was happening, I stood there rigid and frightened.
Miss Potts lowered her eyes for an instant, then
looked up and took my hand. Not passionately.
Gently. As gentle as her smile.

"Would you like to come to my house this evening?" she asked.

"Yes, Miss Potts."

"You won't tell anyone, will you?"

"No, Miss Potts. Honest to God, I won't."

That night we sat in her duplex apartment, shared a
cigarette, talked about school, and listened to some
music on the phonograph. Later, as we sat side by side
on the couch, she said athletics was only a small part
of life, that I should be interested in what was going
on outside of school, and outside of Gary. "Learn,"

she said. "Be well rounded. And don't be discouraged." After that we went into the bedroom and sat down with our arms around each other. Everything got oddly quiet. A clock ticked somewhere. My heart hammered in my throat. A hundred years passed. Then she said in a low, sweet voice, "I'm going to show you what to do."

It was marvelous. She took her time. She made me take mine. She made me feel better, smarter, more aware. An awareness of change swept through my body like a delicious force. Life fell into place. The world was no longer dark and haunted. Miss Potts made me feel like a man.

We became very involved. Almost every day after practice I'd run to her apartment and we'd make love for about an hour. Then I'd run home for supper. Nobody ever suspected. Nobody. It was a wonderful secret, which I've kept until this moment.

On our last day together we went swimming in the lake, then took our blankets and walked along the dunes; away from the beach, away from the picnicking kids and teachers who were celebrating the end of the school term. Far up in the dunes I broke the long silence of our walk and said, "I love you." She put her face up to mine. She seemed on the verge of tears.

We found a deserted cottage and went in. "There was a time when this must have been lovely," she said, adjusting her eyes to the crushed beer cans and solid river of sand that had washed across the flooring. Now, with the door shut, she took off her bathing suit, spread out the blankets, pulled me down, and kissed me hard on the lips. "I love you, Alex," she whispered.

"Then don't go. Don't go back to Ireland."

"I must. It's best this way."

"But you said . . ."

She explained: "When you're in the prime of life, I shall be old. How terrible it would be if we disregarded that fact. Think of it. Can you understand?"

"Sort of."

"Are you afraid?"

"I don't know."

"Well, you shouldn't be. There are so many good things waiting . . ."

A week later she flew back to Ireland. I sent her an airmail postcard.

Dear Miss Potts:

I want very much to thank you for everything you have taught me, not only as a teacher, but as a person.

                              Your student,
                              Alex

Almost two years had passed since my father's death. By then, his insurance money had been used up. We were in financial straits. During the summer, in order to help out at home, Teddy and I worked in the mill. Louie worked there too. He had graduated from Purdue and was going off to play with the Washington Redskins. The Redskins gave him a decent salary, but Louie wanted to make sure we had enough cash around to take care of all the bills that were mounting up. Every payday he'd cash his steel-mill check, take ten or fifteen dollars out for himself, and turn the rest over to mom. A few times she said, "Oh, save it for a rainy day." Louie would have none of it. He stuffed the money in her pocketbook, or in an empty sugar bowl, then went out to have a couple of beers with his friends.

Nick was in the marines. Every few weeks we received a letter from him. He hoped all was well at home and said he'd be writing later.

In the summer Helene gave piano lessons to neighborhood kids whose mothers wanted them to know something more than the further adventures of Howdy Doody. Helene took them in, taught them how to play scales, and "Old MacDonald Had a Farm," and that's how she was able to put some extra food on our table. In the fall she would start her second year at the conservatory in Chicago, but in the summer she gave piano lessons, did most of the shopping, cooked our meals, washed our clothes, and watched over Paulie.

Paulie didn't have to work. He was only twelve. But he ran errands for Helene, made his own bed in the morning, and never complained about anything. In his own way, Paulie helped out as much as the rest of us.

Mom worked the day shift and the night shift at Methodist Hospital. We hardly saw her. She went out in her white uniform every morning. When she came home late at night, all the starch was gone—from her body as well as her uniform.

One summer evening she said to us, "I think we should sell the Chrysler. It's such an upkeep." A few days later Louie drove my dad's car over to the Chrysler dealer and sold it. We loved that car. Now it was gone, like a foolish dream.

The summer faded. Gary nodded in wavy heat. I wandered about the house, grappling with questions that had no answers. Then I'd go out to meet Tony Frank. We'd take long walks down Baodway, listening to the jukebox sounds of Billy Eckstine and Frankie Laine and Nat King Cole; music that oozed like honey from the bars and restaurants. Sometimes there'd be a movie to see, or Tony and I would hang around the pool room until closing time. After that we'd walk back to Connecticut Street, noses pointed to the sidewalk, hands jammed into our pockets, saying nothing to each other because a private war was going on inside me. Tony saw it all. He responded by keeping silent.

One night, while I sat on the front porch, thinking gloomily about my return to Emerson and another season of athletics, my mother came up to me. "What's the matter?" she asked.

The remark, so sympathetically expressed, hit me in the pit of the stomach. It was as if I had been caught in a petty crime.

"I'll be okay."

"I know. But you should learn how to face things."

"Like what?" I demanded, challenging her for a sign, anything that would clear away the fog of indecision.

"Whatever it is that's bothering you. Are you concerned about the future?"

"The future? Mom, you don't understand."

"Maybe not. But remember, school is just around the corner. There's so much to look forward to."

I thought of Miss Potts, and our last day together, when she had vaguely sensed my dread of being left behind, discarded like a broken toy that no longer deserved attention. What was that she had said to me in the cottage? Something about all the good things waiting? Where? With whom? Jesus! Who gives a shit!

I said, "Sure, there's always football."

"If that's what you want . . ."

"The truth is—I don't care one way or the other."

The sweetness drained from her voice. "If you ever

decide to *enjoy* what you can do best, it would make all the difference in the world."

"Why?"

"Because then you'd care."

7. Something's Gotta Give

At sixteen I was in great physical shape, thanks to a muscle-toning summer in the mill. I jackhammered cement until my brain shook, stoked coal in the open hearths, stripped rails, and lifted heavy barrels onto trucks in a ritual of hard, sweat-drenching labor. At summer's end, weighing 185, with not an ounce of fat on my body, I was as strong as I'd ever be in my life.

In September I started my junior year at Emerson High. Teddy had graduated. He was at Purdue University, mainly because Louie—who had distinguished himself there as an All-America lineman—wanted it that way. Teddy packed some things and with a great deal of apprehension went off to play football for the Boilermakers.

Although Teddy wasn't a naturally gifted athlete, he nonetheless pushed and worked like hell to get the recognition that came so easily to Louie and me. While I scraped along in grade school, Teddy held the limelight at Emerson. He had two happy years there. Then I arrived. And stole his thunder. He couldn't stand it. He drove himself unmercifully to catch up, and finally made All-State guard in his senior year. By then I had captured my second consecutive All-State ranking—first as a freshman guard, then as a sophomore tackle. I paid a heavy price for those honors.

Although Teddy would praise me when I did well

on the field, if I made a mistake he'd be all over me, cursing, stomping around in small circles, striking himself on the chest, rapping me on the helmet with stinging results. Through it all, I never mentioned what I'm sure he wanted to hear. No. It would have been too much to openly admit that Teddy was probably the most aggressive high-school player I'd ever seen. Just as it was impossible for Teddy to accept the idea I was at least his equal when it came to playing the line for Emerson. So we stood apart, isolated from each other in thought and deed.

Then Teddy went on to Purdue. And still another Karras joined the Emerson football squad: my kid brother, Paulie, the good-natured one. Always cheerful. Never argumentative. Following my father's death, he leaned over backward to make things easier for all of us. Knowing this, and what I had to go through with Teddy, I inwardly vowed to treat Paulie as an equal during his freshman and sophomore football seasons at Emerson.

I also began serious preparations to be come Emerson's starting fullback.

As a lineman, I lived with the screaming sounds of pain and terror. In the tangle of purple—crimson—yellow—blue—black uniforms, I saw the enemy's eyes, fiery slits that found the terror in my own eyes. I heard the hollow voices, echoing: "You still in here? Goddamn! Sonofabitch! Get off! Get off!" For I was a lineman, and daylight blinked dimly from the far end of a long tunnel. But to play fullback meant a chance to flee from danger. I'd be able to sweep to the outside, or cut to the inside, through the slightest crack, past the swiftest defender—cut and run and be gone into the daylight, where all the glory is!

I told Coach Rolfe about my plans. "If you can get under eleven seconds in the one-hundred-yard dash, I'll give you a shot," he said.

I needed a stopwatch and someone to time me. Tony Frank said he would. One morning just before fall practice began, I took the trolley to Broadway and Ninth and went directly to the Star Jewelry Store. No other store, I thought, contained such treasures, with its gold and silver watches and jeweled bracelets and diamond pendants displayed so temptingly in the front window. Sometimes, on my way to the pool room, or to a twenty-five-cent movie at the Grand, I'd stop to linger there, fascinated by the elegant trinkets that sparkled like a king's ransom in velvet-lined trays. But the daydreams soon evaporated, and I would move on.

However, this time, with twelve dollars in my pocket, I went inside and eagerly approached the jeweler. "I'd like to buy a stopwatch. My friend is going to time me in the hundred-yard dash."

The jeweler grinned, pulled out a tray from one of the counter drawers, and held up an impressive-looking Benrus. "How about this one?"

I fingered the bills in my pocket. "It looks expensive."

"Well . . . it's very accurate. Guaranteed for a whole year." He showed me how to work it. "Simple, isn't it?"

"Sure is."

He squinted at a small white tag on the back. "It'll cost you seventeen dollars."

"Oh. I don't think—would you have anything cheaper?"

"Nope. This is the last one in stock." I turned to go. "Hold on," he said. "How much can you afford?"

"Twelve dollars."

He turned the stopwatch over a couple of times, inspecting my face all the while, as though something was hidden there for him to discover. Then he leaned across the counter and said, "You're one of the Karras boys . . . right?"

"Yes, sir."

"Well, tell your mother Mr. Gress says hello."

"Sure."

"Now, about this watch. I guess I can let you have it for twelve dollars . . . tax included. Okay?"

"Gee, that's swell. Very nice . . ."

On the way home it dawned on me that I had seen Mr. Gress once before—in my father's office. I remembered him grasping dad's hand, gratefully, almost in tears. He seemed so happy, as if my father had just saved his life. Maybe he had.

Anyway, that afternoon Tony Frank and I went over to Gleason Field. With Tony positioned at one end-zone stripe, I took off from the other goal line and covered the 100 yards in just under eleven seconds. A short rest, then off again in the opposite direction; cool air rushing by, turf sliding back beneath my feet, strength and speed propelling me like a thoroughbred toward the finish line. It took exactly 10.8 seconds to get there. And I wasn't even tired!

It went on like this day after day, thinking speed, running all out—again and again—at Gleason Field and on my block, with Tony clocking me all the way. At the first practice of our fall season, I ran under eleven seconds again. So Coach Rolfe, true to his word, switched me from the tackle position to starting fullback. I was elated. It was going to be a sensational year, the brightest of times, the most fun I would have in any of my days in school.

I played basketball that year, averaging over twenty points a game. I played fullback for the football team and led the conference in scoring. Things moved along marvelously. Even my grades, nothing to rave about in the past, got much better. Subjects such as math, history, and biology suddenly became enjoyable. And at sixteen, something else happened. I fell madly in love with Sandy Donegan.

We first met during my sophomore year. Louie was a senior at Purdue then. He was dating her older sister Millie, who lived in Hobart, some ten miles southeast of Gary. One day he asked me to go there with him.

"C'mon. You'll meet Millie's little sister. She's fourteen, and real cute."

We drove to Hobart, a fairytale town of clean streets and white-steepled churches and green lawns with winding paths that led to the front lawns of gleaming colonial homes.

There was a staircase, and the most beautiful girl I had ever seen walked down that staircase. It was as though I had been swept into a technicolor movie and held there by a pair of sparkling blue eyes that belonged to an adorable princess with flawless skin, silken brown hair, and perfect teeth. The sight of Sandy Donegan was overwhelming. When she reached the bottom step, Millie introduced us. There I stood, wearing Teddy's good pants, with the crotch down to my knees, and Teddy's Sunday shoes, which had big knobs in front—Li'l Abner-style. I almost choked with embarrassment.

That evening Louie took us to a drive-in movie. He paid for the show, the hot dogs, the popcorn—the whole works. Then he slithered down in the front seat with Millie. The feature came on: a James Cagney film, with lots of singing and dancing by Doris Day and Gene Nelson. And from the back seat, huddled against the window while Sandy sat an arm length away, I watched Louie and Millie massage the breath out of each other until the screen went dark and dozens of car engines started up. In all that time, I didn't say five words to Sandy.

What a washout I had been. I was too intense, too fidgety. She'd never want to see me again; I was certain of that. All my hopes sank like a stone.

At the front door, Sandy said, "Thank you." I grinned stupidly, slapped her on the back, and said, "See you around." Then I slunk off, turning my head just once to catch her reaction. She looked glum.

"I'm sure glad that's over," I said to Louie as he put his car in gear.

"Don't you like her?"

"Who?"

"Sandy, of course."

"I was boring. Look, let's not talk about it." Louie switched on the radio and hit the accelerator, and we sped north to Gary.

For two weeks I brooded about Sandy. I felt the enormous difference in our lives. She had model looks, elegance, poise—that part of her brought a stab of regret, and pain at my own deficiencies. I wanted to be handsome, gentlemanly, and sure of myself. But I could only fantasize about it all, having no clear idea where I stood with her.

One day I asked Louie about Sandy's father. Louie said that Mr. Donegan had built his career working for the A & P, first as a unit manager, then as supervisor of all their stores in Gary. He was very rich, said Louie.

"How rich?"

"Oh, I guess he makes around fifteen thousand a year."

"That's better than average American, isn't it?"

"Sure is."

"Where are *we*?"

"I'd say somewhere on the bottom of the pile, Al."

Everything runs in cycles, though. I was soon caught up with scholastic sports. Now it was basketball. We had advanced to the sectional playoffs and would be meeting Hobart High at Gary's Memorial Stadium. Sandy went to Hobart. So I telephoned her the night before the game.

"Are you coming into town to see the sectionals?"

"Yes."

"I'm playing forward for Emerson."

"I know. Your brother Louie says you're very good."

"He did? Well, maybe you would like to have a Coke with me after the game, or something."

A pause on the other end of the line. I became agitated. "I want to see you. I like you! We'll have a Coke, that's all. What's wrong with that?"

"Nothing. That would be nice."

"What?"

"I said it would be nice to see you after the game. Are you all right?"

"Of course I'm all right! I mean . . . everything's terrific now."

She laughed. A lovely laugh. The ultimate had happened. She liked me.

The next day we played Hobart. I performed like a magician, blowing their defense apart with a flashy dribbling act and uncanny moves to the basket. I scored more points than anyone else on the court and led Emerson to an easy win before a noisy partisan crowd. But only Sandy Donegan mattered. I spotted her a couple of times, sitting halfway up the seats, enthralled with the action.

At the final buzzer, I dashed down to the locker room, showered in two minutes flat, dressed like someone going to a fire, flew up the stairs, opened an exit door, and pushed my way through a horde of high-school students. Sandy was nowhere in sight. I asked one of the kids if there was another entrance to the stadium. He pointed down the block. I ran, thinking the worst, convinced that I'd done something wrong again, and she wouldn't be waiting for me. But she was. And she looked more beautiful than ever as I rushed up to her side.

She owned her own car. It was parked near the stadium. We drove to a drugstore on Broadway, ordered Cokes, and talked. She told me about her summer in camp, the dance and piano lessons she was taking at a private school, the friends she had, the movies she liked, and so on. After that, I told her how I had gotten my job at the mill. "The mayor of Gary arranged it so Teddy and I could work there after my father died. They were good friends." Then I told her how hard it was working in the mill. "I have to bust the cement and strip rails and bank the furnaces so they won't overflow. Takes a lot of strength," I boasted. She listened in awe.

We finished our Cokes. I reached into my pocket to pay for them. A dime came out, then a nickel. Sandy took a dollar from her wallet and placed it on the table. I said no, I couldn't let her do that. But she sensed the shame, saw the wounded look in my eyes as I kept fumbling for coins that weren't there. "Here," she said, "take the dollar. When you go back to work next summer, you can buy me something."

She drove me home. The porch light was on and we could see some people sitting there, probably neighbors. "You don't have to walk me to the door," I said. Then I went around to her side of the car and kissed her. It lasted a second, long enough for the sensation to pass through me like a comet. I walked up the porch steps in a trance, only half hearing the neighbors as they congratulated me for playing so well in the sectionals.

Sandy and I saw a lot of each other after that. Sometimes I'd get a ride out to her house on the back of Tony Autominelli's motorcycle. More often, I'd have to hitchhike. A few times Sandy drove me home in her car. Then the situation got bad.

Mr. and Mrs. Donegan were Catholic, and they wanted Sandy to associate only with Catholic boys. They were very definite about it. Mr. Donegan, in particular. He was really peeved because his daughter had been dating someone out of the faith. He hardly talked to me at all. He'd just grunt when I came to the house, and then go back to reading his newspaper. So I decided not to go there anymore. Sandy would meet me at the public library, or in front of the movie theater, or somewhere else in Hobart.

It was a lot easier for both of us the next summer. Her brother Don lived in Gary and played football for Notre Dame. Sandy would tell her father she'd be going to visit Don over the weekend. She'd drive to Gary, pick me up at the steel mill after work, and we'd spend a few hours together. Then she'd go over to her brother's house to stay for the night. This happened quite often, but I sensed that Sandy was troubled by the wide gulf that separated us. I could tell. I knew something had to give.

I'm sixteen years old, and an All-State fullback. We've won all our regular season games and will soon be playing Froebel High—a predominantly black school—for the city championship. For almost a week, I've trudged the two-mile distance to Froebel's practice field. Emerson doesn't have a bus to take its players there. But the long, tiresome walk satisfies a desire to be alone with my thoughts. All sound seems to fade away, even the rumble of factory life. Passing through the bleak, garbage-strewn alleys into open daylight, I halt for a moment to light a cigarette. The blue smoke is a symbol, the generator of dreams. The fading spirals also represent pleasures that are past. So I press on; football gear, packed tightly in Louie's old canvas bag, shifting from shoulder to shoulder along the way. The weight of it seems amazingly light, as does the time. Is it an hour? A minute? I can't measure the time. I only know that it has passed, and I'm at Gleason Field, where a rush of noise puts an end to the silence.

It's evening. Supper is being served. I bend over my plate, halfheartedly pick at the food, oblivious of everything going on around the house. The food grows cold. I push it aside. The remains are carried off to the kitchen by my mother. With great self-discipline, she says very little about my bad table manners. The period of strain and tension will continue right up to Emerson's title clash against Froebel. But mom understands. She's gone through similar times with all her football-playing sons.

Meanwhile, my stomach has shriveled to the size of a walnut.

The days drag. And now it's time to play ball. Stepping down from the front porch, bundled in heavy outerwear to ward off a brutal wind, I begin the hike to Gleason Field.

Dusk. A stray dog pads down the street, barking fearfully at dust swirls. A baby cries. The hacking cough of an old rummy escapes from a window. Has it all come to this? Will it always be this way? What is life?

It's too impossibly complicated.

Now a surge of gut-swelling hunger drives me forward to Tony Autominelli's house. That smell! Spaghetti and prosciutto sauce!

The front door is unlatched. I step through and go into the kitchen. The Autominellis have just begun their nightly feast.

"Alex, what's up?" asks Tony's father. Mrs. Auto-minelli turns from the stove, holding a large pot of spaghetti. Even the steam smells good enough to eat. "Ahhh . . . it's you. Take off your coat. *Mangia! Mangia!*"

I pull up a chair and push spaghetti into my mouth as fast as Mrs. Autominelli can dish it out. Tony's father watches, bug-eyed. "Take it easy," he says. "Whassamatta, they starvin' you at home?" He whacks me on the back. "Sonofagun, you want more?"

I consume four pounds of spaghetti, a pint of prosciutto sauce, a half-bottle of wine, and a whole loaf of bread. I can hardly move. But I can see the big brass clock that hangs above the Autominellis' re-frigerator. It's nearly seven o'clock. I'm going to miss pregame practice. No question about it. With a quick wave, I race into the night.

A small fire starts in my belly. I should stop for a while, at least slow down to a fast walk. But I don't. I see the lights above Gleason Field, and the boarded fence, and the barbed-wire top. The fire leaps higher. It moves down my legs; bloated pain spreading like lava in every direction. Thank God! I'm inside the gate.

"Hey, Karras!" yells Art Rolfe as soon as I get to the locker room. "Where the hell have you been? Get into your uniform. Kickoff's in five minutes!"

"But, coach—I have to . . ."

"Are you with me, Karras? I said . . ."

"Okay, okay . . ." There's an involuntary tighten-ing. The queasiness subsides. The crisis has passed.

A clattering rush. We break from the locker room. A few players burst out onto the field as though they've been shot from cannons. The Emerson fans spring from their seats to cheer us on.

I duck down and do some push-ups. When I arise, the nausea has returned. Meanwhile, the marching band has invaded midfield. I wobble to the sideline with my teammates.

> *Oh say can you see*
> *By the dawn's early light*
> *What so proudly we hailed . . .*

Froebel kicks off. The ball carries into the gloomy yellowish lights, lost in the glare. And then emerges— looking as big as the Goodyear Blimp. A curve of electricity snakes down my spine. Jesus! Let someone else get the ball. Oh shit! It's here!

Starting from our 3-yard line, I bolt forward and zigzag up the field; arms pumping, legs stretched, head ringing with the sound of my own voice: *Someone hit me, please!* But Froebel High rolls back like the Red Sea before Moses. There's nothing in front of me. I've broken the sound barrier. Boom! It's a 97-yard touchdown! And I've lost Mrs. Autominelli's spaghetti and prosciutto sauce all over the Froebel end zone.

"Gimme a K . . . gimme an A . . . gimme an R . . . gimme another R . . . gimme an A . . . gimme an S . . . Karras! Karras! Karras! Yea team . . ."

Poor Teddy. He quit Purdue that fall and came home, saying he just didn't like their football program. Underneath it all there was an obvious hurt. No matter how he tried to disguise it, I knew that busted pride had brought him back to Gary, nothing else. At Purdue they expected him to be a younger edition of Louie. They put a lot of pressure on him, and he couldn't contend with it. He had to quit. I think Louie was outraged by the whole thing.

Anyway, Teddy hung around the house all winter,

then went back to school. This time he decided to go to Indiana University, where he played solid football the next fall under Coach Bernie Crimmins, and was happier than he had been in a long time.

8. See You Around, Greaseball

In the spring of 1954 the letters arrived bearing telltale postmarks: Norman, Oklahoma; East Lansing, Michigan; Bloomington, Indiana; Iowa City, Iowa; Austin, Texas; Tallahassee, Florida; Los Angeles, California; Boulder, Colorado; Bowling Green, Ohio; College Park, Maryland—well over one hundred colleges stuffed my mailbox with offers. They wanted me to be a football-playing Sooner, or Spartan, Hoosier, Hawkeye, Longhorn, Seminole, Bruin, Buffalo, Falcon, Terrapin, and so on. It would take a strong effort to ignore any of them, even the inconceivable inquiry made by the Bulldogs of Yale, who obviously had not checked out my grades at Emerson.

The Indiana Hoosiers had an inside track. For one thing, Teddy was playing for them. During the early spring he called me every week or so. "Coach Crimmins wants you down here," he'd say. "What's your answer?" I couldn't give him one.

Toward the end of my final semester at Emerson he said, "Coach is on my back. He's really pressing me. Are you interested in playing for us, or not?" I still couldn't give Teddy a definite answer. "Well, you better come to a decision soon," he growled, "because I don't need all this responsibility."

That was typical of him: always breathing down my neck, trying to shape my thoughts and my life, never asking me what had gone wrong in the process, and what had gone wrong in his own life. I was torn, a breath away from either slamming down the receiver or saying, "Okay, Teddy, whatever you want, if it'll make you happy."

The line suddenly went dead. Teddy had hung up.

Artie Angotti also tried to influence me into going to Indiana University. He owned a string of doughnut shops in Gary. Everybody called him Donuts. One day in late April he came to my house and said he'd give me a job that summer.

"How much do you pay?" I asked.

"Two sixty-five an hour."

"Wow! That's better than I make at the mill. What do I have to do?"

"Stuff jelly into the doughnuts. Softest job in the world—get it? Heh-heh-heh . . ."

Donuts was an alumnus of Indiana University; a big booster of the football team. I had met him through Teddy. In his spare time he combed the bushes for prospective Indiana football recruits. I was one of the most sought-after high-school players in the nation that year, so I imagined Donuts wanted me to go to Indiana in the worst way.

He did. The conversation soon swung over to hard facts. During the summer I would live in his house on the Westside and not leave it except to punch little holes in his "bismarks" (as he called them) for a gross salary of $106 a week. I'd have a fortune saved before going to Indiana University that fall, Donuts said.

"But why do you want me to live with you?"

"Because otherwise," he said with a straight face, "those goddamn recruiters will be around your house every night bothering the hell out of you."

A few days later Donuts sent a crew of professional painters to my mother's house. They stuck up ladders and painted the place from top to bottom. Mom kept asking them, "Why are you painting my house?" She had no idea where they had come from. In another gesture of good will, Donuts bought me a suit, the first one I had ever owned that wasn't a hand-me-down from Teddy. The next weekend I wore it to a dance at Horace Mann High School.

Sandy had enrolled there when the Donegans moved from Hobart to Gary. They bought a house on the Westside, not far from the school. All through the spring Sandy involved herself with new teachers, new schoolmates, extracurricular activities, and helped to plan Horace Mann's spring dance. "Would you like to come?" she asked sometime in April. "There'll be too many swells there," I said. "Anyway, I'm a lousy dancer." I remembered our first date, when I had felt inadequate and out of place in Teddy's clothes. I didn't want it to happen again. Sandy was disappointed, but the best I could say was, "I'll pick you up after the dance." She said I didn't have to—she'd just go on home from there. I said that was fine with me. Then we talked about other things.

On the evening of the dance I decided to surprise her. I put on my new suit and then called Joe Cash. He drove me out to Horace Mann. As soon as the car crossed to the Westside, I felt we had moved into forbidden territory—light-years away from my own universe. It was like going to Hobart. Only, this time I would be rubbing elbows with the cookie-pushers of Horace Mann. Everyone at Emerson called them that. Those were my thoughts as the chiseled façade of Sandy's school appeared up ahead.

Outside the auditorium door a ticket taker stopped me. "You belong here?"

"I'm looking for my girl. She's inside."

The ticket taker wrinkled her nose, started to say something, then let me go in. The auditorium was crowded and noisy. I could see a few teenaged musicians on the stage—skinny-looking kids in dark suits. They were playing loudly above the heads of unfamiliar faces, cookie-pushers in pink and blue dresses and white jackets with bow ties. In the midst of the hubbub a slow but sure hush fell over the floor. A path opened for me. Close to the stage, I saw Sandy and a tall, gawky, redheaded guy with a horsey face. They had their arms around each other, cheeks touching. They were staring straight at me.

The guy's name was Steiner. I had met him once at Don Donegan's apartment. Steiner played football for Horace Mann and planned to attend Notre Dame after graduation. Don filled him in about the team and the coaching strategies, and emphasized that most of the players were practicing Catholics, just like themselves. Steiner smiled when Don said that. Then he sneaked a look at Sandy. I got very peevish and shut up like a clam the rest of the evening. The next day I asked her what she thought of Steiner. She said she didn't think of him at all. He was Don's friend, not hers—why? I dropped the subject and eventually forgot about the whole thing. That is, until I saw them on the dance floor. They looked like newlyweds.

Steiner didn't want any part of me. He immediately disengaged himself from Sandy and stepped back. I took her by the arm and we walked off the dance floor. My head was reeling. I could see nothing but the sight of us on other days: riding horses and going to drive-in movies and drinking Cokes and mowing the lawn in front of her house in Hobart, and wrapping ourselves up in a blanket on a beautiful beach late at night to look at the stars and the moon; lying there talking until we fell asleep. I could tell her anything. Like how scared I was before a ball game. And how happy I was to be with her. She was the only person I could talk to about my happiness and my sadness. I couldn't do that with anyone else. Only with Sandy Donegan. I loved her with all my heart.

Outside the school, I said, "I don't know what your problem is, but I want to marry you."

"Are you sure?"

"Positive."

"I know you mean it." And after a pause: "I hope you don't change your mind, because I want to marry you, too."

"Maybe we'll spend our honeymoon in Florida," I said.

Florida is the Sunshine State. It attracts millions of sun-worshipers every year to its beaches, which include Palm Beach, Daytona Beach, Miami Beach, Fort Lauderdale, St. Petersburg, Clearwater, Key West, and Biscayne Bay. But in the late spring of 1954 I didn't know any of these places. To me, *all* of Florida was one, big, beautiful beach.

Anyway, a line coach down at Florida State University had kept a regular correspondence going with me after I had been selected as an All-State player for the fourth year in a row—a record-shattering achievement in Indiana high-school history. In early June I received a round-trip plane ticket from the coach, along with a brief note: *Greetings from the Sunshine State. Will meet you at the Tallahassee Airport.*

What an opportunity! I'd never been out of Gary, except to nearby towns like Hammond and Muncie and Fort Wayne, and once to Chicago for my cousin's wedding. When the time came for me to board the plane, all I could think of was how wonderful it would be to swim in the ocean and lie on the beach, with the sun shining all day long.

It was raining when the plane landed. Down at the foot of the ramp I could see this huge man. He must have been six-nine, weighed close to 300 pounds, and had great big muscles on his arms. He was the Florida State coach, looking intently at the door of the plane. Confidently, I stepped down the ramp to greet him. But he kept looking over my shoulder, apparently looking for an enormous guy with three suitcases under each arm to emerge and straighten up seven feet tall—that's the guy he expected. Well, I weighed 200 pounds, stood six feet even, and carried no luggage. So I had an almost uncontrollable urge to turn around and get back on the plane. But I walked up, punched him lightly on one of his bulging arms, and said, "Hi coach. It's me, Alex Karras." He looked down and blinked, incredulously, as if he had just met Spanky McFarland of the Little Rascals.

He drove me to the Florida State campus and said nothing during the entire trip. But his face was full of misery.

For five days I hung around the campus, all alone, while a dozen other high-school phenoms were being wined and dined, and dated up with pom-pom girls, and driven around in big Cadillacs provided by Florida State's athletic department. I spent most of the time in my room, not even going out for dinner. Nobody cared. I didn't see the coach again until he took me out to the airport for the flight home. A few players from around the country came along with us for the ride. They laughed and kibitzed while I looked out the window into a murky drizzle, thoroughly disgusted with Florida and everything I had gone through. At the airline ticket counter I stuck my hand out. "I want to thank you for the five days, coach."

"Sure, kid."

"Only, there's one thing that bothers me."

"What's that?"

"You never did ask me if I could play football."

I moved into Donuts's house that June. Every day I operated a little machine in the back of his shop, squeezing jelly out of a nozzle into the doughnuts. I must have filled six million that month. In early July mom called and said my Emerson class ring had finally arrived in the mail. So I asked Donuts if I could borrow his car and go home for a few hours. "Sure," he said, "but don't talk to strangers."

That afternoon I met Sandy at Eastside Park. We sat down on a bench and I gave her the ring.

"I guess it's too big for your finger," I said. "But you can have it sized."

"Oh, no. I'll get a nice chain and wear it around my neck."

"Swell. Anyway, I'll soon have enough money saved to buy you a diamond ring. There's one in the Star Jewelry Store window. It's really beautiful! ..."

"This will do fine," she said, looking at the ring as though it was the nicest gift she had ever received.

One evening, unexpectedly, Sandy came over to Donuts's house and asked me to go for a walk. She led me straight to Louie's house. Four men were sitting in his living room—three coaches from the University of Iowa and a private-airplane pilot. After ten minutes of conversation, Louie put his hand on my shoulder and said, "It'll be best for the family if you go to Iowa." I didn't question him. His word was law.

There was a quick ride to the Gary airport. A few hours later I ended up in a little town close to where the Ocheyedan and Little Sioux rivers cross in the northwest corner of Iowa. It might as well have been in Colorado, because Louie never mentioned the state I was flying to. Neither did the Iowa coaches or the pilot. The only thing they told me was that I'd be staying with a Jewish couple by the name of Shine, who lived in a town called Spencer. They would put me up in their home for the summer. "Ben Shine is an Iowa alumnus," said Louie. "You'll be okay there. But don't call anybody. Not even Sandy. You understand?"

"In other words," I said, "it's just like Donuts's all over again, right?"

"Not exactly," chuckled Louie. "I understand Ben owns a matzo factory."

I believed him.

When I got to Spencer, I discovered that Mr. Shine owned a junkyard in town. He also raised sheep. His barn was always filled with wool. He said that he had made a lot of money in the wool business, but I never did find out what he did with all that junk. Anyway, he and Mrs. Shine were lovable people. I admired and respected them both. They treated me just like a son.

Mr. Shine gambled. He would gamble on anything, usually for high stakes. Crapshooting was his specialty. One evening he took me to his country club. It was the first time I had been involved in really heavy gambling. The members apparently had nothing else to do in that club except shoot craps. I saw hundreds of dollars change hands on every pass. I stood at the table and watched, absolutely astounded. After a while, Mr. Shine asked me if I had ever played the game. "Yes, sir. Since I was three years old." He gave me a fifty-dollar bill and invited me into the action. When my turn came, I put the fifty dollars on the table, closed my eyes, threw the dice—and crapped out.

Every day at the Shines' seemed too good to be true. I fished, took long walks, ate hearty meals, and watched a lot of television in my own private room. Of course, I kept my end of the bargain with Louie and stayed away from the phone.

Meanwhile, back in Gary, the people from Indiana University had placed a stakeout in front of mom's house. Every so often Donuts himself would ring her doorbell. "Is Alex in?" he'd ask. Her only answer was a plaintive cry: "He's gone . . . where is he . . . do you know?" Fortunately, Louie made sure that mom understood my absence was caused by a recruiting war among the colleges, and that one of them had me safely hidden away from the rest. "As soon as Al registers, he'll come home," Louie assured her. Otherwise mom would have had every cop in Gary dragging the bottom of Lake Michigan for my body.

Teddy took a terrible mental beating that summer. He didn't know where I was, either. And Bernie Crimmins didn't believe him.

On an August day, duly registered as an Iowa freshman, I walked across the campus to a gigantic field house and saw a whole army of football players there. Like myself, they had gathered from the power high schools of New Jersey, Pennsylvania, Ohio, Wisconsin, Indiana—from everywhere—hoping to play for the Iowa Hawkeyes in the Big Ten Conference. All of them were big; the majority, All-Staters.

On command, we lined up in a long, straight row. Then one of the coaches said, "All three-year All-Staters step forward." About ten stepped forward. The coach looked down the line again, and said, "Any four-year All-Staters here?" I saw the oblique glances and heard whispered comments of disbelief as I stepped out—the only one to do so. It had been almost two months since my last visit to a barber shop. The hair was over my ears. I had on Levis and a stained Indiana University T-shirt and carried two pairs of pants and Teddy's black double-breasted suit over my arm. I guess every other football candidate in that field house thought I was the least likely among them to be a four-year All-Stater. Maybe I looked like a gangster, or what a gangster was supposed to look like in those days. I don't know. But Bob Flora must have thought so. He was Iowa's line coach; a bald-headed man who had a doughy face and carried about 250 pounds of blubber on his six-two frame. He walked up to me a few minutes later and said, "Okay, you pool-room bum, get checked in with the counselor."

I blinked. Then he jerked his head up and down, ran a finger around his shirt collar like it was strangling him, and said, "See you around, greaseball."

That was my introduction to college and the better way of life.

In early September I went home to Gary. It should have been a great day; a reward of some kind. Instead, the punishment went on. I had arrived on the train early in the afternoon, went directly to my house, answered all the questions that mom could throw at me, then called Joe Cash.

"Will you take me to the Westside?" I asked. "Sandy's still in school. We'll be able to get there before classes let out. How about it?"

Joe said okay, but he didn't seem very enthusiastic.

On the way to Horace Mann High, he said, "Sandy's still seeing Steiner."

"Where'd you get that from?"

"At the mill. Someone told me."

"Who?"

"Some guy who knows Steiner."

"Yeah? Well, it's bullshit."

"Might be . . . I sure hope so."

I made him stop the car a block from the school. "Wait here," I said.

When I saw her, she was walking slowly down the steps with Steiner. He had his arm around her waist. I ran up to them. Steiner let go of Sandy, glaring at me with bitter eyes. I hit him with my right hand and knocked him flat. Then I ripped the graduation ring from Sandy's neck. "You didn't care enough!" I shouted at her, squeezing the ring in one upraised hand with all my might.

That evening she came to my house, remorseful, swearing she'd never see Steiner again. She said nothing had changed. She still loved me and always would. I gave the ring back. We kissed and clung together for a long time. It was easy to do. I had become too well acquainted with sorrow and torment by then. For me, making up with Sandy was like getting used to a frequently reopened wound.

A few days later I returned to the University of Iowa. Shortly after that, Sandy enrolled at a swanky school in Lake Forest, some forty miles north of Chicago.

9. Nothing in God's World

Memories of my first days at the university: the clear Iowa River running between the campus and dormitory gounds; oak and maple and hickory trees lining the walks where students stroll on their way to class; the old administration building, with its pillared dome gleaming in the autumn sunlight; all kinds of birds—bluebirds and redheaded woodpeckers and robins—perched on cottonwood branches down by the river; a solid line of Canadian geese passing across the eastern sky along the Mississippi flyway to nesting places in nearby cornfields; taking a deep breath on a country road without coughing. These are the remembrances held of some better moments in my freshman term at the University of Iowa. I was no longer an Emerson schoolboy, but I had not yet become a man.

The worst moments were spent in class. The courses—math, social science, foreign language, communication skills—seemed far over my head. Instead of taking notes, while the professors talked, I'd play tic-tac-toe in my notebooks. In math, it became so embarrassing that I just left the room one day and didn't show up until the very end of the term. So, I flunked the final exam and had to take the course all over again during the summer.

There's a story behind what happened at that final

exam. I had a friend named Phil, a tall, lanky kid, somewhat on the homely side—but he came from a decent family and rooted for the football team and knew I was very big with all the waitresses in the student cafeteria. Phil was an engineering major and a real genius in math. He just *loved* the subject. He always got straight A's. Well, I was having such a horrible time with math that I went to Phil and asked him to take the test for me. "If you take the test," I said, "I'll fix you up with one of the waitresses." He had an awful case of acne. He couldn't get a date with anyone, so he became terribly interested in the proposition.

"What do I have to do?" he asked.

"Nothing to it. We'll go to the exam together. You'll sit down and I'll sit down. I won't write anything on my test paper. You put my name down and take the test. Just make sure you get a C, not an A. Otherwise they'll think I've cheated. Besides, all I need is a C to pass the course."

Phil was scared to death. For a week I had to keep conning him about the waitress in order to build his confidence.

Finally the day of the math exam came. We went in together. There were at least six hundred students taking the same test. When we received our exam papers, I whispered to Phil, "Sit in the back. I'll take a seat up front. When the test is over and everybody's crowding around, we'll transfer papers."

The test started and the students started to scribble away. I played tic-tac-toe on my paper, all the while thinking about the great C Phil was working on in the back of the room. With three minutes to go, I heard this assistant professor—who'd been stalking up and down the aisle looking for cheaters—I heard him say in a very loud voice, "Phil, what are you doing in this room?" Not a bad question, considering that Phil was an advanced engineering major and into things like nuclear physics and the theory of relativity, which made him very popular in the math department. And here he was taking a test not much more advanced than simple arithmetic.

I saw Phil jump up and run out of the room. He took off like a big dog was chasing him. What could I do? I handed in a test paper that was filled from corner to corner with tic-tac-toes.

The math department had Phil under fire for days, but he managed to stay in school. I never got him laid. Come to think of it, I believe he went through college without ever getting laid.

That autumn Iowa had 110 freshmen on football scholarships; more than enough players to go around in the daily practices. Wally Swank was our freshman coach. I liked him. He was low-keyed, easy to talk to and get along with. Anyway, Swank divided us into teams. Every day the Black played the Blue. We put a lot of effort into the drills, hurling ourselves full out for an hour and a half before Swank called a halt to the proceedings. Occasionally we'd scrimmage the varsity, and we more than held our own. We were that good. I was a standout on the freshman line—way in front of everyone else in that department—blocking and tackling as though I had been born for it.

Bob Flora was too busy coaching the varsity linemen to be around me much that fall. However, every time our paths crossed, he'd say, "Hello, greaseball," or, "What do you say, Pool-room Johnny?" He always said it with a tremendous smile on his face, but not a smidgen of humor showed through. It irritated the hell out of me. Nevertheless, I swallowed hard and took the insults without retaliating.

Calvin Jones, then a great All-America guard for Iowa, sensed my discomfort, for he had heard Flora's crude eruptions more than once on the practice field. "Don't let it get you down, man," he said to me one day. "If Flora thought you was shit, he wouldn't be mouthin' off like he does." Coming from Calvin Jones, the words did wonders for my battered pride. I admired him right off the bat.

Calvin was a big black guy, strong as an ox, and one of the nicest, gentlest souls I've ever known. He came from the steel-mill town of Steubenville, Ohio, where he had worked his high-school summers in dust-clogged factories, doing the same kind of things I did in the Gary mills. We had a lot in common.

At that time, like almost always, I had very little money to spend on the necessities of life. Calvin soon developed an unerring instinct about my circumstances and, because we had hit it off so well during those first practices, one particular morning he asked me about my eating habits. "You gettin' all you want?"

"No. I can't afford anything more than hamburgers in the cafeteria."

The next time I saw Calvin he gave me enough meal tickets to keep me in steak and roast beef the rest of the week. That's the kind of guy Calvin Jones was.

Meanwhile, fall classes dragged on—one more boring than the next. But I did enjoy the physical-education courses, which included gymnastics, tennis, volleyball, and some other sports that I had never participated in before. They helped to keep my grades up to a passing level.

Then a lull. Thoughts of Sandy dragged through my head, spreading unbearable loneliness in their wake. For days I sat in my dormitory room, speaking to nobody, feeling as glum as any loner could possibly be.

The end of a cool, golden fall turned into a freezing winter. On weekends, with football over, with studies too difficult to contemplate, I'd hitchhike from

Iowa City to Lake Forest in brutal weather to see Sandy. I still loved her. There were problems, sure, but she said her parents would somehow accept me even though I wasn't Catholic. "They know you're going to college and trying to get somewhere in life," she said to me during those weekends in Lake Forest. "Just be patient. Everything will turn out okay."

I scraped up enough money to buy her an engagement ring; money that had come from my summer job in the doughnut shop, the remainder from the nickels and dimes I had put into a savings account while I worked for USS.

One morning, after phoning to say I wouldn't be going out to see her that weekend, I changed my mind at the last minute and took to the open road, hitchhiking east from Iowa City, waiting in a Davenport diner for hours to catch a milk truck into Chicago, and going on from there to the Evanston city line. I was dropped off in the bitter cold. I had to walk in deep snow to an all-night gas station, where I thawed out until daybreak. Then I caught another ride all the way to her school.

She wasn't in the dormitory. One of the students, who had never seen me before, said Sandy had checked out for the weekend. "She went away with a friend."

"Was his name Steiner?"

"Nope. Another guy. They're kinda stuck on each other, I guess. Why? Do you know her?"

I heard the door slam behind me, and I remember running through the snow and then taking a bus to Evanston, and then waiting four hours at the railroad station for the train to come in and take me back to Iowa City. It was almost dark outside when I found a seat.

A sudden pull, the slow screeching of wheels, the chug-chug-chugging over tracks; houses going by

. . . and factories . . . and ribbons of light, and telephone poles, farmland, hills, horizon, sky, stars.

I wept. When the tears dried up, I swore that nothing in God's world would ever cause me to show that side of myself again.

10. Evy

The wound healed. And I found a sponsor.

Every freshman at Iowa had one. They came with the territory; affluent businessmen in the area who acted as Good Samaritans to the athletes, asking nothing in return except to be "in" on the Big Ten scene—particularly with the daily happenings of Iowa Hawkeyes football. My sponsor was Ernie Pannos, a movie-theater owner with a fondness for foreign art-films.

He gave me my first job in college as an usher in one of his theaters. I spent eight hours a day watching all the big hits from Europe. Actually I got my foreign-language credits—French and German—through that theater experience. The subtitles helped tremendously. Naturally, I had to concentrate when the actors spoke, though if I missed a line or two they were bound to say the same thing all over again.

Ernie devised a way for me to pick up two easy credits in another subject. He had a friend, an art professor at Iowa. The professor maneuvered me into his sculpture class. My only responsibility was to get into the class before the other students, go behind a sliding curtain where the clay was kept in a wooden box, put on a rubber apron, water down the clay so that it looked just right and proper, and dig out a lump for every student as they came by. That was my job. Nothing to it. After handing out the clay, I'd leave and have a couple of Cokes in the cafeteria. The professor said I was doing fine. "You're the best clay mixer I've had in years," he said. "Keep it up and you'll get a B in the course."

For six weeks this went on. One day, after I had handed out the clay, a beautiful girl in a raincoat came in. She had long auburn hair, high cheekbones, a full mouth—a beauty. I'd noticed her before, though she'd never come by for a lump of clay. This time she did, and said, "I'm late."

"What do you do?"

"I'm the model."

She unbuttoned the raincoat. It slid from her shoulders to the floor. She was *nude!*

So I shoveled out two big lumps of clay, dashed into the classroom behind her, then watched as she stepped onto a platform and struck a pose. Cripes! The students had been sculpting her for *six weeks* and I didn't know it! I took over a table right in front of the platform and started working on my lump of clay. No more Cokes in the cafeteria for me! No more clay mixing, either. I became an *anatomical sculpture* student like everyone else. And I got a B in the course.

One other thing about that class. After I had finished the sculpture, it looked just like a frog. So I painted it green and shipped it home to mom in an eggcrate. She put it on the coffee table in our living room. When the neighbors came around and asked, "What's that green thing on the table, Emmy?" she'd say, "That's Al's frog." She was very proud of it.

By now the stir and excitement of campus life had struck a responsive chord. Determinedly, I made plans to pull my grades up by passing the math course in summer school. So I went home for a couple of weeks after the spring term to work in the steel mill in order to pay the tuition. While there I almost got killed.

It happened on the midnight shift. I had fallen asleep on a stool. Somebody screamed and I woke up just as a billet fell from overhead. Luckily, I tilted over backward. The billet hit the stool. If I had gone forward, I would have been killed.

I returned to Iowa in mid-June, took the math test over, and passed it. In the meantime, Calvin Jones and I became roommates. When the best freshmen were moved up to practice with the varsity that spring, Calvin played right tackle and I played right guard. Everything would have been perfect if Bob Flora hadn't harassed me with his asides. Almost every practice he'd be sure to say something like: "Nice going, greaseball"; or, "That's the way to do it, you pool-room bum." One afternoon I started spouting back at him. Head coach Forest Evashevski overheard. He came over and wanted to know what was wrong.

I spoke slowly but emphatically. "I'm sick and tired of being called a greaseball and a pool-room bum! I wasn't raised to be called that by Flora or anyone else. If it happens again, coach, I'm packing my things and clearing out of here."

Evashevski smiled. "Okay, Karras, let me handle it." He took a hard look at Flora, then proceeded to chew him out in front of the players. I thought Evy was one heckuva fellow for standing up like a man.

Still, I felt the need for hometown friends, like Big Mesho, who was working in the mill back in Gary. He had played darn good football at Wallace High, but the recruiters overlooked him and that torpedoed his chances for a free college education. He just didn't have the grades to qualify on his own. Anyway, just before I went back to Iowa, we were having a couple of beers at a Broadway tavern and Big Mesho said his life in the mill was terribly hard. "If only some college would give me a football scholarship, maybe there'd be a way to escape from all this drudgery," he said. I had an idea. "Let me talk to the coaching staff. I'll tell them you're as good as me." Big Mesho slugged down his beer and said, "Go ahead. Talk to them." But as we called it a night, he muttered something about trying to get a better job at the mill that fall. So I knew he didn't hold out much hope for Iowa.

A miracle! The Iowa coaching staff took my word. They granted Big Mesho a full football scholarship. I met him at the train station. We hugged each other and jumped up and down like little kids. Then we got on a bus and Big Mesho talked nonstop all the way out to the university. I sat and took it all in. Just then I felt the whole world was wonderful again.

We were roommates for a year. The other players started to call us "Ike and Mike" because we looked alike. Later, they switched it to "The Tons of Fun." It got to be hilarious. We did a lot of crazy things. I'd be in my room, and there'd be a knock on the door. I'd open it and *splash!* Big Mesho would score one for his side with a bucket of water. Our room looked like a public swimming pool. We had an inch of water on the floor all the time.

There was a premed student from Hawaii. A real bookworm. He had a room between us and two other guys that were feuding with us. Every night we had a water fight with the guys, and the premed student would hear all the noise going on and think someone wanted to see him—maybe one of his professors—so he'd stick his head out and *whack!* he'd get hit with a bucket of water, first from one side and then from the other. We had him in a constant crossfire. He was always wet.

Big Mesho and I did other things that weren't very constructive. We sneaked into movie theaters, sneaked out of restaurants without paying our checks, hung out in bars until three in the morning, then slept until noon and missed classes. Finally, the carousing got us into trouble with the authorities. We had come in drunk late one night and started another water fight. A security officer rushed down the hall. "That's enough. The floors are getting warped. Any more of this and you'll be kicked out of the dormitory."

A couple of nights later we came in drunk again, and spent some time with a basketball player we knew. He was seven feet tall. We borrowed his overcoat and hat. Then I climbed on Big Mesho's shoulders and put on the coat so that it hung down over both of us. Pretty soon there was an eleven-foot man walking down the hall in a big hat. Big Mesho reached out of the coat and thumped on the dormitory proctor's door.

He was a little fellow, a sort of Wally Cox character—Mister Peepers—who weighed about 83 pounds. At first there was no answer. We waited, swaying back and forth, until the door opened. The proctor had a silk bathrobe on. From Big Mesho's shoulders I could see his eyes fluttering. He *slowly* looked up and saw me looking down at him from under the big hat. His mouth fell open; out came a tight little scream. "Eeeeeee!" Big Mesho panicked. He started running down the hall. I shouted, "Look out!" But he couldn't see a thing from under the coat. He ran me straight into a huge crystal chandelier, which must have been more than a hundred years old. It fell down and shattered into a billion pieces. We got kicked out of the dorm. Big Mesho found a one-room apartment and I moved in with Ernie Pannos.

Then it was September, the start of my sophomore year. I reported to first practice about twenty pounds overweight. Forest Evashevski wasn't too happy about it. He had heralded me to the press as a sleek, hard-as-nails lineman. One who was going to rank among the nation's finest players. And there I was, a starting tackle before the first game had even been played, already in a jam with the head coach.

Evashevski had had the good fortune to play for the University of Michigan from 1938 to 1940, when the gifted Tommy Harmon (a Gary, Indiana, native) was his teammate. Evashevski blocked and opened the holes. Harmon ran through them. He ran wild, scoring a total of thirty-three touchdowns in his college career and winning the Heisman Trophy as a senior. Harmon and Evashevski: a legend in college football history. Evy made the most of it.

The very first time we met, he brought "the good old days" at Michigan into the conversation. Right after we said hello. "I used to block for Tommy Harmon," he said. Then he went into a prolonged account of the great games he and *Tom* had had against Ohio State and Yale and California and so on, getting into intricate details about the formations Michigan used. I hardly knew what he was talking about. It sounded like some weird code.

Another impression of Evashevski. He had a low basso voice. It rolled from his chest like thunder and scared the hell out of people. Once, when he cut it loose on the practice field, I looked up at the sky and waited for raindrops to fall.

Evy became the Iowa head coach in 1952. His team won only two of nine games that year, then improved to a respectable 5–3–1 record in 1953, and went one game over the break-even mark in 1954. Evy claimed his 1955 team would do much better. He predicted that Iowa would be primed for a shot at the Big Ten crown, and might even sweep to its first national championship in thirty-four years. Those were his public statements. The fact of the matter is, away from the press he saw a betrayal of trust in many of the players who had reported for practice. He complained: this receiver is too slow; that safety is too awkward; such-and-such running back is too dumb. And Alex Karras, his starting tackle, is without a doubt too goddamned fat. "You better get the lard off," he said after I stepped down from the training-room scale.

Evy had Bob Flora run me in place for half an hour every day after practice. He blew a whistle to stop me and start me. I hated the whistle. But Flora enjoyed blowing it. He had an evil grin on his face, like he was playing a part in a Nazi torture film, with me as the victim.

We played our toughest game against the University of Wisconsin. They pushed us all over the field and won. Badger guard Bobby Konovsky was opposite, and he inflicted the worst physical beating I'd ever taken. I was helpless out there, pathetically inept. But Flora didn't yank me from the game. In the locker room, I anxiously looked at my right ankle. It was swollen three times its normal size. The trainer injected it with Novocain. Then Evy walked over and said I had stunk out the stadium.

"Well," I answered woefully, "why didn't you put somebody else in?"

"Don't tell me what to do," came the angry reply. He looked at the ankle. "Seems like you have a simple sprain." Then he walked away.

Some sprain. The bone was cracked. But no X rays were taken. I limped along on it for weeks without ever knowing the true extent of the injury. Meanwhile, Flora kept blowing his ridiculous whistle on the practice field. He blew it so hard the veins in his neck stood out while I ran in place, with the pain shooting up from my swollen ankle to my groin and then down again. Adding insult to injury, Evy demoted me to second string, then to third string. Finally, he benched me. I didn't mind that so much. The ankle was still sore and swollen. I could hardly walk on it, let alone play. Yet, the reason Evy gave for taking me out of the lineup made no sense at all. He said I had a defeatist attitude. Because of it, our football team had fallen on its ass. That was his reason! It was ludicrous. I just couldn't believe it. We began squabbling all the time after that. He ranted and raved about my so-called lousy attitude. I yelled back that I didn't like his. Through it all, the only thing that kept me from quitting Iowa was the thought of Louie—his rage—how terrifying he'd be if I crawled home to Gary and told him I couldn't take the punishment. So I hung on.

Toward the end of the season we went down to play Notre Dame in South Bend. I hungered for that game. My mom was coming down to see me, and so was Louie and my neighborhood friends and the guys in the mill. I just *had* to play. No two ways about it. I emphasized it to Evy a dozen times at least. "My ankle feels a lot better," I said. "I can play all out. Give me a chance, will you?"

Evy said he would.

Well, the second-string tackle had been nursing a slight injury, so Evy moved me into his slot just before kickoff. John Burroughs, our starting tackle, got hurt in the third quarter. In spite of this, Evy kept him in. With two minutes left to play, and the score tied, Burroughs was still in there, his teeth clenched as if something was going to snap inside him. I knew he had to come out. I waited. Evy looked down the bench at me a couple of times but said nothing. He deliberately kept this poor, injured kid in the game.

With seconds to go, Notre Dame's Paul Hornung kicked a field goal. We were beaten, 17–14. That was it for me. I decided I would quit Iowa, even if it meant Louie wouldn't talk to me for the rest of his life. Damn it, I thought. I'd rather work my tail off in the mills than go through the humiliation of another season under Forest Evashevski.

In the steamy, congested dressing room, Evy asked why I was so pissed off. "Burroughs shouldn't have been out there. He was absolutely dying from pain," I snarled. "Why didn't you put me in?"

"Well, Karras, to tell the truth, I never really thought of it."

I threw my shoe at him, got my clothes, and went home.

For days after, mom begged me to go back to Iowa. Not Louie. He said, "You made your bed, now sleep in it." I couldn't sleep a wink. Then the phone rang. My sponsor, Ernie Pannos, had some bad news. "Evashevski has taken away your scholarship," he said.

"It doesn't matter. The way things look, Ernie, I may go to the University of Tennessee next fall. I can get a scholarship there."

It was the truth; Tennessee's recruiter had been checking back and forth with me for almost a year, knew the situation at Iowa, and guaranteed I'd get a much better shake down in Knoxville.

"Don't do anything you might regret," said Ernie. "Let me tell you the good news."

I listened. If I'd come back to Iowa, Ernie would finance me through the spring term and also pay for any courses I might have to take over in the summer. Then, if I made Iowa's football team in the fall, Evashevski would reimburse him. Ernie was willing to take the risk that I'd make the team. He felt I wasn't a quitter. "What do you say, Al? Will you do it for me?"

How could I refuse? He was a wonderful man. He

had been good to me; no strings attached. I loved him dearly. So I said okay.

I lived at his house in Iowa City that spring. In the summer I made up another math course. To help take some of the financial load off Ernie, I got a job painting the university's Kinnick Stadium. It had sixty thousand wooden seats. The custodians gave me a bucket and a long brush. I went out to midfield, looked up at all those seats, and right there I coined the phrase all stadium painters use to this day: "My God, where do I begin?"

In September 1956 Evashevski threw me into the "hamburger squad," aptly named because our only function was to scrimmage aginst the varsity, using the plays that Iowa's opponents would employ against them during the season. I did well enough to work my way into the fourth varsity squad, which didn't even travel with the main unit. In our scrimmages against the regulars, I was ferocious—obsessed with the desire to do what I had to do in order to become Iowa's number-one tackle. Evashevski was impressed. Taking a giant step forward, he promoted me to third string.

In our opener that year we went against Indiana University. Teddy captained the team. I wanted to play opposite him. The only trouble was that Evashevski had other plans. He'd use his regulars; nothing less would suit him as he prepared to take on the Fightin' Hoosiers. I found a way to solve the problem. The wrong way.

Our second-string tackle had a bad knee. I knew it. During one of the scrimmages that preceded the game a ball got loose and a pile of guys began to swoop in on the halfback. I drew a bead on the tackle's knee and ripped ligaments. That ended his career. It was the most vicious thing I ever did on a football field.

At the final big scrimmage, I made thirty-five single tackles in front of a large crowd of Iowa boosters. Evashevski got so filled with enthusiasm he promptly announced that I would be starting aginst Indiana.

The newspapers made a big thing out of it. One headline read: KARRAS BROTHERS TO MEET HEAD-TO-HEAD IN HAWKEYE-HOOSIER OPENER.

The Marchin' Hundred Indiana band in Bloomington's Memorial Stadium stirred the fans during pregame ceremonies. My heart leaped when Teddy and his teammates came through the rotunda in their cream-and-crimson jerseys for the warmups. It was that kind of moment: sweet, tremorous, and breathtaking—all rolled into one. But just before kickoff—with mom and Louie somewhere in the stands—Evashevski hollered, "Burroughs!" And Burroughs jumped out to start in my left tackle spot.

I almost died. A cold rage grabbed hold and stayed there during the first series of plays. Then Evy yanked Burroughs and sent me in. I played fifty-eight minutes—offense and defense—and slaughtered whoever played opposite me in the Indiana line. I just killed them. Meanwhile, Teddy held down the Hoosier left guard position, so our publicized head-to-head confrontation didn't take place. Personally, I was delighted. Or maybe I should say . . . relieved.

We beat Indiana, 35–0. Afterward Evy came over to congratulate me. He stuck out his hand. I brushed it aside, still in a violent mood because he had sent in Burroughs. I told him so. Without batting an eye, Evy said, "I wanted to test you."

"*Test me?* What is that supposed to mean?"

mean, Karras, it was done strictly for psycho-
easons—to see if you had any guts."

I came off my stool. "Take that psychological crap and flush it down the toilet—you rotten sonofabitch!"

The next day I took off for Gary, on the verge of a nervous collapse. It was that bad.

A week later Evashevski called. He apologized. I told him I would go back to school only on the condition that he and Flora would not talk to me for the rest of the season. *Not one word.* "Okay," he said. If that's the way I wanted it, he'd go along and just let me play my game. So I got on the train and went back to Iowa. Evy stuck to his promise. He kept Flora off me, too. They never talked to me again that season.

The arrangement worked out fine. I made All-America in the major polls—Associated Press, United Press, International News Service, *Life* and *Look* magazines—and Iowa won the Big Ten championship.

All this happened, but my personal life continued to slide downward. I had almost no interest that year in what went on during classes. I seldom spoke to the other players. I didn't care for girls anymore. And when Big Mesho was kicked out of school I felt more lonely than ever. The loneliness seemed to sum up all the struggles in my life. I was ashamed of it.

Still, there was a very important matter to take care of. Evy had not yet fulfilled his obligation to reimburse Ernie Pannos for my tuition and lodging. It came to two thousand dollars. So I went to see Evy in his office. "I want Ernie's money," I said.

To which he replied, "There's no possible way. I just can't do it."

I leaped over his desk and wrestled him to the floor. "I'll kill you!" I hollered, and meant it.

My fingers tightened around his throat. Just then, Bob Flora burst in, pushing and shoving to get me off him. It ended up with the three of us fighting like Hollywood stunt men, knocking down file cabinets, overturning chairs, crashing against the walls. It was idiotic.

But I got paid. Evy gave me everything he owed, and I turned it over to Ernie Pannos.

A few days later the team went out to Pasadena to play Oregon State in the Rose Bowl. We won by a big score. One other thing. I had thirty-seven tickets for the game. The day before, a man called me at our hotel, saying he was an Iowa alumnus and would take the tickets off my hands for one hundred dollars apiece. He gave me an address where I could meet him. It was a bowling alley. "I own it," he said. "Putting up another one in Malibu next month. Sixty-four lanes."

I ran into the place counting up the money in my head. The man took my thirty-seven tickets, excused himself, and said he was going into his office to make out a check.

I waited an hour. Then I asked around. Nobody had heard of him. He must have gone out the back door, said the real owner.

Such is life.

11. A Lion Roars—Meow

I had an opportunity to go on a big, glorious trip to Greece.

It took some doing, but I finally convinced the Chicago chapter of the Order of Ahepa to sponsor me as a shot-putter and discus thrower for a Greek-American track team that would be competing in the Balkan games. I had never hurled the discus. Not once in my whole life. And my best shot-put effort had been a mediocre forty-eight feet, made during high-school days. They sent me over anyway, because of my football reputation.

On a July morning in 1957 we sailed tourist class out of New York, the Manhattan skyline fading as we began the eleven-day trip across the Atlantic to Athens. Sprinkled among the other passengers were twenty-four airline stewardesses. There were parties every evening; anonymous people having a good time on mountainous seas with the waves pounding and my own head pounding from too much liquor and not enough sleep.

We docked in the harbor of Piraeus, five miles from Athens. Soon after that I climbed up sixty marble steps and looked down on the city, at a great crescent of handsome public buildings and broad boulevards leading from a central square to the foot of the Acropolis. At the top, kings and scholars and warriors lay dead and buried under 2,500 years of history. But their broken temples were still upright.

And then a visit to the Hall of Records, where I found a log with the family name on it: KARRAS. The literal translation from the Greek is "black horse." One of the officials—a bent-over little man with a gray beard—thought it might have happened this way: *Long before the days of Homer, the Karras tribe had crossed the Mediterranean from Africa to the Ionian island of Kefallinia. There, they tilled the soil and grew olives and vines, and suffered through a civil war, and then sailed to the Greek mainland, to be slowly absorbed, down through the centuries, in speech and customs by the Minoans, later the Persians, the Macedonians, and then the Romans.* "I think maybe . . . like this," he said in halting English. "No matter. Karras name never change. Is Greek from beginning."

I thanked the official and left the building feeling great. Just great. An hour later I was in a tour bus, on my way back to the Acropolis, where Plato and Aristotle and Karras had once walked and pondered the complexities of an evolving civilization. I couldn't wait to get there.

I spent six weeks in Greece. There was a girl—I think of her often. Her name was Kristina. She sang at the Astoria Hotel in Athens. A brilliant girl. At eighteen, she spoke sixteen different languages. It was amazing. She'd talk to the hotel guests in their native tongue and, at the same time, bowl them over with her beautiful looks. Such eyes. They were so bright, so filled with innocence.

I stayed at Kristina's apartment for three weeks. Mornings I'd get up and go to the stadium for practice. Afternoons we'd take strolls through the old-city marketplace and eat in the outdoor cafés. We also visited the National Archaeological Museum, because Kristina said she had a strong interest in ancient history. Early evenings I'd watch her get dressed for her singing job at the hotel. After that I'd wander around the side streets of Athens, doing very little of anything until it was time to pick her up at midnight and take her back to the apartment. Those were fun times. We always had something to laugh about.

One morning I told her of this weird fantasy I had had during my second trip to the Acropolis. "I saw myself making passionate love to a beautiful goddess on the steps of the Parthenon," I said. Kristina thought it was a very healthy fantasy. She wanted to know if I thought it should be fulfilled. "Oh, yes," I said. "With you, and nobody else." We laughed about it for ten minutes.

On her night off we took a taxi to the Acropolis, walked up the steps, and went directly to the Parthenon. There, under darkening skies, we took our clothes off and started to make passionate love between two marble pillars. Then the spotlights came on and the entire Acropolis could be seen from miles around. I have no idea if anyone saw us from the nearby hotel balconies, but it didn't matter. Kristina and I made love until my fantasy had been thoroughly fulfilled.

The last time we saw each other was at a party—a great big bash thrown by Aristotle Onassis on one of his beautiful yachts. Anyone who was *anybody*, and anyone who was *nobody*, attended—royalty, millionaire business people, movie stars, writers, artists, athletes, unemployed people, drifters, beachcombers, bums—name it; they were there. Everybody wanted to be around Onassis. He welcomed us all. He came into the dining room, made a short speech in Greek and English, then walked over to the tables. I was thrilled when he shook my hand and wished me luck in the

Balkan games. Then Kristina and I started to drink with the others. Pretty soon almost everybody got drunk. The bartenders and waiters kept filling our glasses and we went right on drinking until four in the morning. By then, I was so out of it that Kristina had a tall, handsome guy in a tuxedo take her home. Right after that, I passed out. It was the wildest party I'd ever been to. A few days went by before I screwed up enough courage to go to her apartment. She wasn't there. The landlady said she had taken a singing job in Salonika, way up north. She wasn't expected back for a month. So that ended it between us.

The Balkan games came to an end, too. I threw the shot fifty-four feet and placed third in the event. Then I developed a mysterious back injury. I couldn't compete in the discus throwing. Thank God.

The first week in September I returned to Iowa and began my senior year, playing on an even better football team than the one we had in 1956. But the Hawkeyes couldn't generate enough offense to win when it really counted. Unbeaten Ohio State clinched the Big Ten championship and went to the Rose Bowl. Still, on a personal level, it had to be my most rewarding season at Iowa. I made All-America again and won the Football Writers' Association of America Outland Trophy as the most outstanding lineman of the year. Out of all this came my first appearance on national television.

Jack Lescoulie, host of the "Today Show," had me before the NBC cameras for a full ten minutes. I said some very corny things. "Without the big guys up front the little guys can't do it. . . ." Things like that.

But I'm getting ahead of myself. At the start of the fall term, I picked up where I had left off in the spring. Once again I was the campus misfit. I couldn't have cared less. All those self-assured, solid undergraduates out there—male and female—would only say hello and try to be friendly while it was convenient to exploit me for their own special reasons. As an example: although I had never joined a fraternity, the Sigma Nu members on campus would invite me to their frat house in order to show me off to the new pledges. "Meet Alex Karras, All-America tackle," they'd brag to the initiates. I'd shake hands with the pledges and mumble something about the "wonderful spirit that permeates here at Sigma Nu." Phil, my old math-exam buddy and president of the Iowa chapter, coached me on that particular phrase. And a few more, besides. So I served a purpose. In the meantime, it was a decent way for me to get an occasional free dinner at the frat house.

Then came a fateful day. I was in the student bookstore, trading two of my books for ten dollars in order to have meal money for the week. It seems I always had to wind up in the bookstore doing just that. When I ran out of books, I'd distract the clerk and steal them back from under his nose. It was a vicious circle. Anyway, the point is—while we were making this big transaction, a tall, leggy blonde walked by. She had it all.

"Who's that?" I asked the clerk.

"Joanie Jurgensen. She's a sophomore."

"Oh, my . . ."

Where have you been all my life, beautiful Joanie Jurgensen? Oh my, where in the world have you been?

The Sigma Nu held a big party a couple of weeks later. I was there, drinking beer and eating triple-decker salami sandwiches in a corner, when she came in with one of the friends of Phil, the mathematical genius. It took an hour before I could get up enough nerve to speak to her. "Hello," I said. "My name is Alex Karras."

She smiled sweetly, extended her hand, and said, "Pleased to meet you."

I turned to a pillar of salt.

The next day I inveigled her phone number from Phil. Then I called.

"Remember me?"

"If you tell me your name, maybe I'll remember."

"Alex Karras. We met at the Sigma Nu party."

"Are you the one who was eating all those sandwiches?"

"Yeah . . . that's me. Listen, would you care to go out tonight?"

"All right."

"There's a nice restaurant we can go to. I mean—you can eat anything you like."

I met her at the girls' dormitory, wearing my Iowa football jacket, Levis, a little plastic hat—a beanie-looking thing—and white-buck shoes. She looked me up and down, and I felt like an idiot.

Ernie Pannos had loaned me his car—a Hudson convertible—and we got in and drove to the Wagon Wheels, an off-campus hangout for the Iowa students.

Almost every night I'd be in there, not talking to anyone; drinking six, seven, eight bottles of beer until I threw up. Then I'd go home deep in the dumps, wishing there were other things to do in life except play football and get drunk at the Wagon Wheels.

Anyway, Joanie and I ate fried chicken there on our first date. I had only one bottle of beer. She drank a glass of red wine. And we talked some.

She grew up in Clinton, Iowa. Her father was the vice-president of a savings bank and an executive at the Clinton Corn Processing Company, a division of Standard Brands. He also owned a bowling alley. The Jurgensens were well-to-do, all right. I could see that without Joanie having to tell me about her background. She ate the fried chicken with a knife and fork, not with her hands—like I did. She was bright. She knew what was going on in Washington, and in the rest of the world.

When we left the Wagon Wheels it was raining. So we quickly got into Ernie's car and drove back to the campus. On the way, I told a joke. It fell flat. I tried another. She didn't get that one, either. I tried to remember some more, but gave up trying. Then we were in front of her dorm. The rain pounded on the convertible top and fogged the window. We sat for a while and I finally thought of something to say.

"I don't want you to think I'm pushy, or anything, but the top is leaking."

"Um."

"It's coming from right above your head."

"Funny. I don't feel anything."

"Well, it's dripping slowly. I think you should move a little bit closer."

I put my arm around her shoulder. Then I kissed her on the cheek.

The rain stopped. She got out of the car and waved good night. There was nothing left to do except drive back to Ernie's house. But I decided to sit and think about things for a while. I must have sat for an hour. I sure had plenty to think about.

In December 1957 I had a pretty fair idea of who I was, where I came from, and where I was bound. In the last instance—to the National Football League. And specifically, to the Detroit Lions, who had just selected me as their number-one pick in the college draft.

But who were *they?* And where did *they* come from? Well, before long I would surely be a small link in the long chain of Lion history, so it made sense to find out a few facts about the organization.

Pro football came to Detroit in 1925 when the NFL granted Jimmy Conzelman a franchise for fifty dollars. He coached and quarterbacked the team—then known as the Panthers—to a third-place finish behind the Chicago Cardinals and Pottsville Maroons. Conzelman lost a bundle at the gate.

He tried again in 1926. The club finished twelfth in a twenty-two-team league and then folded. There was no pro football in Detroit the next year.

In 1928 ex-Michigan All-America quarterback Benny Friedman started up the Detroit Wolverines. Friedman played quarterback and Leroy Andrews was the coach. After winning seven out of ten games, the Wolverines drowned in a sea of red ink.

There was no pro football in Detroit in 1929, and for four years after that. In 1934, a radio-station owner by the name of George A. Richards bought the Portsmouth Spartans for $21,500, transferred the club to Detroit, dubbed them the Lions, and selected Potsy Clark as head coach. The team landed in second place behind the Chicago Bears.

A year later the Lions went unbeaten in their last four games to edge the Green Bay Packers for the Western Division crown. Then they played the New York Giants for the NFL championship, and won, 26–7, on first-quarter touchdowns by Ace Gutowsky and Dutch Clark, and last-quarter touchdowns by Ernie Cadell and Buddy Parker. Twenty-seven Lion players earned $300 apiece in prize money.

In 1936 the Lions placed third in the Western Division. In 1937 Dutch Clark replaced Potsy Clark as head coach.

In 1940, George Richards sold the franchise for $225,000 to Fred Mandel, a Chicago department-store owner. Mandel then brought back Potsy Clark as head coach. The next year Bill Edwards took over Potsy's job. John Karcis replaced Edwards the same year. And Gus Dorais directed the club for the next five years. But the Lions still couldn't duplicate what they had accomplished back in 1935.

On January 15, 1948, Fred Mandel sold the Lions to a syndicate of Detroit businessmen, headed by D. Lyle Fife, an electrical engineer, and Edwin J. Anderson, a brewery executive. Fife was elected president, Anderson vice-president. Then Bo McMillin was hired as the new head coach. The club opened the season with people like quarterback Fred Enke, two-way back Bill Dudley, tackle Russ Thomas, and middle guard Les Bingaman—who had an oversized stomach. One day, during a practice break, one of his teammates yelled, "Move around, Bing, you're killing the grass." The Lions won only two games that year.

Then came 1950, and the arrival of Bobby Layne, the quarterback who could do everything. He had been drafted out of the University of Texas by the Bears in 1948, then spent one year sitting on the bench as an understudy to Sid Luckman and Johnny Lujack. The next season he operated behind a weak New York Bulldog offensive line. But he learned how to eat the ball, throw it for touchdowns, and run it in on the backs of stumbling blockers. And he made up plays in the huddle by scratching pass diagrams in the dirt with his finger. If his teammates didn't hustle, he scorched their ears with his fire-and-brimstone tongue. This converted them from a bunch of losers to fighting contenders. In the lineup, along with Layne, were three highly touted collegians—Notre Dame end Leon Hart, Southern Methodist halfback Doak Walker, and Colorado A & M tackle Thurman McGraw. Also on hand were halfback Bob Hoernschemeyer and offensive guard Lou Creekmur, plucked from the ranks of the disbanded All-America Football Conference.

Then, in late December, Buddy Parker was named Lion head coach, succeeding Bo McMillin. In a break-even year, Parker declared he was all set to make a run for the league championship in 1951.

In 1951 the club just missed the title by losing to San Francisco in the last game of the season. The next year there was a playoff win against the Rams, then a showdown contest against the Browns. Doak Walker, out most of the schedule with injuries, provided the winning edge when he broke loose for a 67-yard touchdown run in the third quarter, which gave the Lions a 17–7 victory and their first NFL championship in seventeen years.

In 1953 the roster was made even stronger with the addition of rookie guard Harley Sewell, rookie tackles Charley Ane and Ollie Spencer, rookie linebacker Joe Schmidt, and rookie halfback Gene Gedman. The season ended with another NFL championship win. Again, the Browns were the victim. In the final two minutes of the game, Bobby Layne hit Jim Doran with a 35-yard touchdown pass, and Doak Walker kicked the extra point to insure a brilliant 17–16 victory.

The Lions won their third consecutive conference crown in 1954, but crumbled in the championship game against the Browns, losing by a score of 56–10.

In 1955 the club carried on without the services of Les Bingaman, Thurman McGraw, defensive back Bob Smith, and linebacker LaVern Torgeson—all retired after the 1954 season. And Bob Hoernschemeyer and Doak Walker played out their final year, while Bobby Layne played with a crippled arm—the result of an off-season riding accident. The Lions went into a dive. They hit last place in the standings.

Bobby Layne's shoulder healed in 1956. Meanwhile, rookie Hopalong Cassady of Ohio State averaged 4.3 yards in rushing, and Joe Schmidt developed into one of the most feared linebackers in pro football. Blazing hot, the Lions went into the final week holding a half-game lead over the second-place Chicago Bears. But disaster struck when Chicago's Ed Meadows plowed into Layne with a blindside tackle, forcing him to the sideline with a concussion. The game turned. Chicago won, 38–21.

Now it was 1957. A couple of days before the first exhibition game, Buddy Parker got up at a Detroit boosters' banquet and shocked his audience into silence. "This team of ours is the worst I've ever seen in training," he said. "I can't control it. I can't coach it. So I'm quitting. As a matter of fact, I'm leaving Detroit tonight." The next day, assistant coach George Wilson took charge of the club. On the roster were a few talented rookies: Steve Junker, receiver from Xavier; Gary Lowe, a defensive back from Michigan State; and John Henry Johnson, a fullback from Arizona State. During the season, Wilson effectively alternated ex-Packer Tobin Rote and Bobby Layne as the quarterbacks, and moved other players around like an international chessmaster. In spectacular style, the team marched to a conference playoff contest in San Francisco against the 49ers. The date was December 21, 1957.

I was in Kezar Stadium that Sunday afternoon, a guest of the Lions. On December 28 I would be playing in the East-West Shrine Game, on the very same field. But for now I concentrated on pro football.

I watched the 49ers take a commanding 24–3 lead in the first half, then add three more points early in the third quarter. Then I watched Hugh McElhenny, the great San Francisco halfback, carry the ball on a long gainer down to the Detroit 2-yard line. The situation looked hopeless. But the Lions held, took possession, and went on a scoring rampage that didn't stop until they had bolted down the Western Conference title. The final score was 31–27.

Nick Kerbawy was the Lions' general manager at the time. A month earlier, he had congratulated me for being their top draft choice. After that, nothing happened. Not another phone call, or a letter, or anything else from the Lions. I became anxious.

Kerbawy called just before I left Iowa for the Shrine Game. "You'll have credentials to sit on the bench during our playoff against the Forty-niners."

"Thank you, sir. But what about my contract?"

"Don't worry, son. The Lions have big plans for you. So just relax and I'll be seeing you right after the game."

Terrific! We made arrangements to meet, and then I called Louie, who was working for the Firestone Rubber Company in Gary. We went back and forth, throwing numbers around like Wall Street millionaires. After a few minutes of this, Louie still wasn't sure what kind of money I should ask for. "I don't know," he said, "I made thirty-five hundred my first year with the Redskins. If you try for twelve thousand . . ."

"Oh, God."

"And a ten-thousand-dollar bonus . . ."

"Oh, God, Lou. They won't give me that much. I don't want them to get mad at me."

"Well, ask for it anyway. We'll negotiate from there."

I went to San Francisco, and heard rumors that the incomparable Bobby Layne had been getting only $15,000 as a Lion quarterback—and this was his tenth year in the league! It really set me back. But Louie had been through the pro football wars. If he wanted me to dicker for more money than Layne was supposedly getting, who was I to argue?

Kerbawy saw me the day after the playoff. He sat down in my dormitory room and immediately took some legal papers out of his valise. It was the first time I had ever been alone with him. He was in his forties, a peppery guy with short-cropped hair; very executive-looking, right down to his manicured nails. The only thing I knew about him was that he had once been the sports-information director of Michigan State before joining the Lions. Be that as it may, his mannerisms reminded me of a gamecock. He was in his chair one second, out of it the next; talking a blue streak about important people he knew around the league, and elsewhere. "So I said to Harry Wismer . . ." he'd say, and "Jerry Ford called me from Washington . . ." and "William Boyd told me this . . ." and "Danny Thomas told me that . . ." That's the way he came on. Hot. Quick. Exciting. And, eventually, strictly business.

"Well, son," Kerbawy said while I leafed through the contract, "we have a fine ball club. We're always contenders. There's a great tradition behind us. So the time has come for you to seriously think about your future. What kind of money do you want?"

"Twelve thousand."

Before I could spit out the bonus figure, Nick Kerbawy gathered up his papers, put them in his valise, and headed for the door. Then he turned. "I'll tell you what, kid. You should think about playing up in Canada. It's lovely country, you know."

"It is?"

"Sure. There's only one problem."

"What's that, sir?"

"The snow is up to your ass in June."

As soon as he left, I called Louie. "You better slide

the price down," he said. "If you don't, I can't think of anything else you can do at this time of your life."

I went back to school after the Shrine Game. Two weeks later I signed with the Lions. They gave me $10,000, which included a $1,000 advance. That took care of the "bonus."

One other thing. If I didn't make the ball club, I'd have to return the advance.

12. Automatic Otto

While I was negotiating with the Lions, Big Mesho drifted back to Iowa. He had saved up enough money to be readmitted for the spring term, with the proviso that he'd be on his best behavior. Which is just what happened. But it didn't do Big Mesho much good as far as his personal life was concerned.

I had been steadily dating Joanie for two months, and wanted to marry her. I popped the question one night while we were eating at the Wagon Wheels. There was a long silence, and then she said, "We're both so young. Besides, how do you know if you can support me?"

"Easy. I can always make money. The Lions are paying me ten thousand dollars this year. And next year..."

"Maybe there won't be a next year. I mean, what if you get hurt? What then?"

I didn't know. But I convinced her that nobody could hurt me so bad I'd have to give up playing football. So we talked some more, and finally Joanie said she'd marry me. That weekend we drove out to Clinton to see her parents. I was sure her father would be against me. I could hear him saying: "Marry my daughter? You? A poor Greek kid from Gary? Over my dead body!"

But Mr. Jurgensen didn't say that at all. The only thing he wanted to know was: "What are you going to do for a living?" When I told him, he said, "Fine. You have my blessings." I felt as if a ten-ton weight had dropped away.

The day Big Mesho arrived on campus, I broke the news to him. He looked crushed. "Are you kidding me?"

"No. I'm really going to marry her, Meesh."

That stopped him for a second. Then he said, "This whole conversation is stupid. Let's go have a couple of beers."

"Okay, but not now. I'll see you at the Wagon Wheels tonight."

I went there with Joanie and introduced her to Big Mesho. After the food and drinks were served, Joanie told him about our plans to marry in the spring. "Good luck," he said. Then he slugged down a full tankard of beer in one gulp and excused himself from the table.

"What's wrong with him?" Joanie asked. I didn't know how to answer her.

For weeks after, every time Big Mesho and I got together, it was like a scene out of *Marty*. "Let's go to the Wagon Wheels and pick up a couple of waitresses," he'd say. "C'mon. We'll do our little thing with them."

"Listen, Meesh, I told you—I'm off that crap. I'm getting married, man."

"But why?"

"Because I'm in love. I've been telling you this over and over. Don't you understand?"

"No, I *don't*. It just doesn't make sense. What is it with you? You want to marry her because she's a blonde, or something?" Then he would say, "You know, Al, you're getting to be a real drag." And he'd walk away, pissed.

Well, Joanie and I were married in the spring. We had a small ceremony in Clinton, just the immediate families and a few friends. Big Mesho was there, too. He stood up for me as best man.

After the reception, Joanie and I drove three miles to the Bluebird Motel for an overnight honeymoon. Then it was back to Iowa City, where we rented a two-room apartment above an Italian restaurant. We moved in with the bare essentials. The next morning I told Joanie I had to earn some money during the summer. "There's a guy who wants me to wrestle," I said. "I'm going to give him a call."

His name was Pinky George, a Greek promoter who lived in Des Moines. We had met during a Hawkeye football game. Pinky said I could make a lot of money in the wrestling game. So I got in touch with him.

He introduced me to an old wrestler named Chest Bernard. Chest must've been seventy years old. And his chest was no longer the great chest it used to be. But he was a crafty competitor. About six weeks after he had taught me most of the basic holds, I was ready to start wrestling in public. Pinky set up the bookings, with Chest as my only opponent. On weekends, we'd drive up to Chicago, and Canada, wrestle there, then move on to towns such as Dubuque, Des Moines, Moline, Rock Island, Hammond, and so forth. Chest didn't talk much during the trips. He'd usually sit in the back seat of the car, with his arms folded around his sunken chest and a faraway look in his eyes. One time I asked him why he never said much. "It's a lonely profession," he answered.

I found out for myself one night, after a match in Rock Island. Chest said he wanted to stay in town, so I headed home by myself in below-zero weather. About twenty miles out of Iowa City, one of the tires went flat. For more than an hour I tried to replace it with a spare, but my hands were so cold I had to give up. I walked up and down the highway, hoping to wave down a car. No luck. And not a house anywhere in sight. I was surrounded by miles of cornfields. With dawn breaking, a patrol car pulled over. The cop found me huddled in the front seat under an old army blanket. He fixed the flat and I got home at seven in the morning, almost frozen to death. It hurt just to knock on the door.

"Who's there?" Joanie answered.

"It's me. Open up."

"Not until you tell me where you've been all night."

"It doesn't matter where I've been. Open up. I'm about to turn into a cake of ice."

"I am *not* opening this door until you have an explanation."

I took five steps back and charged. The door sprung open and I walked straight past Joanie to the bedroom. Then I pulled the covers over my shivering body and fell fast asleep.

She never questioned me again about my nocturnal wanderings.

The wrestling act was tightening up, getting better all the time. I was the hero and Chest played the villain. So Pinky tagged me with a nickname to go along with the image: Baby Face.

Chest and I worked in some crummy spots. One night we went through our routine in the basement of an old barn, with cow manure falling through the floorboards onto our heads. And once, while we were wrestling in Moline, Chest accidentally kicked me in the eye. It blew up something awful. The crowd loved it. And somebody in the front row began to sing:

> *Baby face, baby face*
> *You've got the cutest*
> *little baby face . . .*

Everyone joined in. Even Chest Bernard. I didn't mind. There were only a couple of matches to go on the tour. By then, my wrestling income had come to nearly twenty thousand dollars. Not bad for a kid still going to school.

That spring I was selected to play for the College All-Star squad against the Lions, who were the defending NFL champions, having beaten the Cleveland Browns at Briggs Stadium the previous December.

Otto Graham was the All-Star coach. In his college days he had played tailback for Northwestern University. Then he switched to quarterback at North Carolina Pre-Flight. In 1946 he signed a contract to play for the newly formed Cleveland Browns of the All-America Football Conference. Under head coach Paul Brown, he became a precision passer. The fans called him Automatic Otto. He could also run. Like a gazelle. His favorite play was the quarterback sneak, in which he'd fall back to pass, then reverse himself and spring loose straight down the middle. Nobody ever worked the quarterback sneak better than Otto Graham did.

I didn't like the man. To me, he was another Forest Evashevski: humorless, intense, consumed with football concepts and very little else. Graham treated all football players alike. From a distance. In his coaching philosophy there was no consideration for an athlete's emotional stress. So we didn't get along while I was with him at the All-Star camp at Evanston, Illinois.

That aside for the moment, I guess the team was as good as any ever assembled. We had guys like Jerry Kramer, John David Crow, Bobby Mitchell, Ray Nitschke, Wayne Walker, Johnny Sample, Jim Taylor, Lou Michaels (my roomie), Gene Hickerson, Bobby Joe Conrad—and me as the defensive captain. The general spirit was high, and we believed that we would beat the Lions in the twenty-fourth annual Chicago classic on August 15. However, my mental attitude was worse than poor during our first day of practice. I had reported to camp with a strep throat and a touch of the flu. I showed up for practice the next morning because I felt I had to.

Graham worked us under a hot sun for two hours, brought us back after lunch for another two hours, followed it with a light scrimmage, then called in the defensive line for more work. "All right!" he barked. "When I blow this whistle, you guys will start to run. When I blow it again, you fall down. Then I'm going to blow it once more. You will all get up and start running again. Get it?"

Like I've said, I hate whistles. Because they're symbols of authority and subservience. So I started to walk off the field.

Charlie Krueger, the Texas A & M defensive end, seemed startled as I broke ranks. "Where y'all goin', boy?"

"I'm going in."

"Ooo-wee, I'm just startin' to sweat," he cackled. "Ah love it."

"Well, you stay here and sweat. I'm leaving."

Graham ran up as I headed for the locker room. "What are you doing? Get back on the field!"

It was now or never. So I said it. "I don't have to take your shit. I'm going to Detroit. And if I don't make it in Detroit, that's a different story."

Graham squared his shoulders. "You can't do that. We're paying you to play here. . . ."

"Yeah? Well, you can take your hundred and fifty dollars, your All-Star jersey, and your blanket with the All-Star emblem on it, and your fucking whistle, and jam them all up your ass!"

And I'm in the locker room.

In the evening I began to pack. Don Doll came into

my room. He had played defensive back for the Lions in the early fifties, and was now an assistant coach at Southern California and an aide to Graham for the All-Star clash. He said that Graham was upset but would forget what had happened that morning if I stayed in camp and cooperated. "Be a nice guy," he said. "Stick it out. If Otto files a bad report, the Lions won't be pleased."

So I stayed. But Graham didn't forget. At Soldier Field, our defensive team lined up and I wasn't among them. I squirmed on the bench until a couple of series had been run. Then Graham sent me in. I played most of the game after that, and really took it out on Stan Campbell, the Lion guard. Everytime he held me, I punched him or cursed him. I was mad, crazy mad. I knocked Bobby Layne down, and hurt him. I knocked Tobin Rote down, and hurt him, too. I used abusive language on all the Lions. I wasn't a nice guy.

We won the game, 35–19, racking up more points than any All-Star squad since the rivalry began in 1934. Before seventy thousand fans, quarterback Jim Ninowski of Michigan State threw two touchdown strikes to Bobby Mitchell of Illinois; West Virginia linebacker Chuck Howley intercepted a Bobby Layne pass and ran it back for another score; Bill Jobko, the Ohio State linebacker, sacked Tobin Rote in the end zone for a safety, and Texas A & M halfback Bobby Joe Conrad kicked four field goals. As for the Lions, they put together three touchdowns on a Tobin Rote-to-Jim Doren touchdown pass in the first quarter, Gene Gedman's touchdown run in the third quarter, and Ralph Pfiefer's plunge in the last quarter. And our guys blocked two Bobby Layne tries for the extra point.

Graham saw it as a great victory. In the locker room he said, "I only wish we could do this all over again. What do you say, guys?"

And everybody yelled "Fuck you!"

Early the next morning I checked into the Lions' training camp at Cranbrook with Wayne Walker, where I met head coach George Wilson. It was the start of a beautiful friendship. The main reason, I suppose, was Wilson's faith in me. He never demanded much; only that I should give full attention to the game while it was being played. The same thing with practice, which seldom ran more than an hour and a half. And when I was away from the football field, he reckoned it was none of his business. Wilson felt that if a player wanted to smoke, drink, or carouse, that was fine. As for curfews, he kept everybody loose. "I guess you fellows know how to take care of your bodies, or you wouldn't be here," he'd say. "And I figure you're all over twenty-one and know the difference between right and wrong. So have a good time and be ready to work when the time comes."

That was George Wilson. A man who had the kind of respect few coaches enjoy. A respect that goes way beyond that which coaches like Vince Lombardi had from his players at Green Bay. Lombardi was effective, I'll concede, but there's no question in my mind that I would not have been able to play for him. When practice was over, and the game was over, I had to be left alone. Lombardi bridged that sensitive line with his players. Wilson didn't. He left *everybody* alone.

13. A Strange World

What goes into the memory of a pro football career?
How much do I remember of that time? Those
players? Those coaches? What happened to the rush
of stadium scenes, training-camp incidents, and long
hours spent in hotel lobbies and airport terminals and
cocktail bars? And in cars that bumped along on
roads no longer traveled by me? There's so much to
remember, and an image is already formed of some
faraway place called Cranbrook, where I see myself
singing the Iowa fight song on top of counters, in the
bathrooms, in the showers. Cranbrook is where I
shined shoes, and fetched towels, and ran all kinds of
errands. Cranbrook. Where I stare in wonder at a
legend called Bobby Layne. And feel the iron in his
voice as he roars with laughter and pounds the dining-room table so hard that plates jump and the
toughest rookies flinch in their seats. I see him now
and remember the scene:

"Hey, rookie," he says. "Y'all think you're something? Hell, you're nothing but a rookie who don't
know enethang. You understand?"

"Yes, sir, Mr. Layne."

"From now on, rookie, you just follow me around
like a puppy dawg. You understand?"

"Yes, sir."

He liked me. He called me Puppy for a few days.
Then he changed it to Tippy. Pretty soon all the

veterans called me Tippy Toes, because Layne thought it fit.

Now I think of him at practice and remember the way he'd grind his jaws, then spit, clap his hands, and bring the guys into a huddle. "Awraht, men," he'd yell in that back-country Texas twang of his. "Let's git it going, heah? Snap. Snap. Make it count." Then he'd go to work, and never break a sweat. And I'd reel around under the sun and wonder what I was doing on the same field with him.

He was the baddest-best pro football player of my time. He feared nobody. Sooner or later he'd find a weakness in a player and capitalize on it. Invariably. It might take him two periods, or three, or into the final seconds to get his points when he absolutely had to. He would often throw short decoy passes, just to see the defensive reaction. When the victim—a cornerback, tackle, linebacker, somebody—broke down once too often, Layne knew exactly where to strike. Bam! It was as though he was riding on the pulse of unnatural movement, propelled by an invisible force.

That was Bobby Layne, the player. I didn't know him too well as a man. Maybe nobody did. Not altogether. But once, while I was chauffeuring him around and he was in a drunken stupor, he told me a story. When he was a kid, about nine or so, he and his father were driving down a country road, and the car turned over. His father was killed instantly. He spent the whole night sitting by that upside-down car with his father inside, until they were found.

I waited a few minutes before Layne spoke again. Then he suddenly said he didn't like the dark. He was too scared to sleep, he said. We were headed for some bar in Pontiac at the time. It must've been two in the morning. Layne's eyes were wide open. And wild.

I was his personal chauffeur. Following the afternoon practices he'd holler for me in the dormitory.

"Hey, Tippy! Let's git some Cutty!" He'd drink nothing but Cutty Sark Scotch. We'd drive to bars like the Bar-B-Que, or the Town and Country in Pontiac, and Layne would drink five or six Cutty Sarks and then I'd drive him back to Cranbrook for the evening meal. After that, we'd go right back to Pontiac again and he'd drink Cutty Sark all night. He made me drink with him. I never drank Scotch in my life until I started to run around with Bobby Layne.

One night, after the Cutty turned me into a sick drunk, Layne drove back to camp, singing at the top of his lungs while I held my head in my hands. He was singing "Ida Red." That was his favorite song. He sang it over and over. Pretty soon I looked up and saw that he had his right foot up on the dashboard, the left one stuck out the window. And while he was singing, I noticed that the accelerator had jammed. I checked the speedometer. The needle shivered at one hundred miles per hour, and we're roaring down the expressway with things shaking and bouncing inside the car. All the while Layne's singing "Ida Red, Ida Red." So I finally got down off the seat, and on my knees I begged him to stop the car. But we kept moving down the expressway with his feet still in the same position and a look of contentment all over his face.

By some miracle we made it back to camp. A few nights later I woke up shaking like an epileptic. From then on, I drove the car—no matter how much Cutty I had in me. Even if I had to rest my chin on the steering wheel and drive six miles an hour. We'd come home with the sun sliding up over the horizon and climb through a window into our beds. I'd get an hour's sleep before breakfast. And Layne would be in the shower, singing. I couldn't imagine how he did it.

Sunrise. The start of activity in camp. Athletes

wiping the sleep from their eyes and filing into the Cranbrook dining room. Athletes eating and talking and slowly building up their stamina. Morning practice. A time to throw off concern, worry, and all thinking about home and family. Nothing to think about except making the club, sticking through the first cuts, and the second. That's all that mattered to me during those first few weeks in camp. Well, I made it, mainly because George Wilson liked having me around. If there were any other reasons, they escape me.

I didn't play much in the early exhibitions. Then I started to catch on and played against the Bears in Norman, Oklahoma; the first and last time both teams met in a preseason game.

Jimmy David was our cornerback. He got smacked in the mouth. All his front teeth fell out. Then David broke Harlon Hill's jaw. And somebody dislocated an elbow. And Gil Mains lit into the Chicago center, who had picked up a fumble, and twisted the poor guy's ankle around until the bone cracked. It was the most brutal game I'd ever been in. Eleven players were carted off the field. And the Bears' public-relations director had a heart attack and died on the plane going home.

Cranbrook on a late summer night. What do I hear? Crickets. A car motor. Laughter down the hall. Coughing. Tinny music in another room. And the sound of my breathing. Then nothing. All is quiet. The pain is gone.

I wasn't aware that the coaches were unhappy with Layne. When he got on the field, it was *his* field. He owned it. The coaches would work out precise diagrams on the blackboard, which were copied into the playbooks for study, and then Layne would come out for practice, spit into the wind, and tell the coaches,

"Y'all advise that end over theah to break it off about two more yards. Heah?" Or he'd say, "Now, George, when that boy makes an outside cut, y'all tell him to take it fahv more yards deep." The coaches went along, because they knew Layne was the best quarterback in the game.

Wilson was using as many young players as possible in the exhibition games. It was hard to tell what the final makeup of the club would be, but I could sense there was a rebuilding program going on. That came by just looking into the eyes of the veterans. On a thirty-five-man squad, twelve rookies remained after the fifth and last game of the exhibition season. The defensive team was more or less as it was the year before, with me filling in behind Gil Mains. The offense, with Layne as our leader, seemed solid enough. We had good outside receivers, strong backs, and a powerful line. So the 1958 Lions were set to make another run for the championship.

We played our opening game in Baltimore. Bobby Layne missed an important field goal when he scuffed the pitcher's mound. After that we gave up. The next week we tied Green Bay in a game filled with lost opportunities. The next day the Lions *traded* Bobby Layne and fullback Tom the Bomb Tracy to the Pittsburgh Steelers for quarterback Earl Morrall and two draft choices.

The whole team went into shock. It just didn't make sense. Bobby Layne was gone. And for me, a security blanket had been ripped away. Funny thing, though. I really didn't know why.

In utter disarray, we staggered around for a few days, then played the Rams at home. They shellacked us. Then Baltimore beat us at home. We flew to Los Angeles after that, and won. But we lost in San Francisco. In San Francisco, Gil Mains picked up a slight injury, so I played more than usual, and didn't dis-

grace myself. At least, George Wilson thought so. He
started me when we faced the Browns in Cleveland.
The Browns. It was Paul Brown's club, then. They
had Jimmy Brown, Lou Groza, Willie Davis, Chuck
Noll, Bobby Mitchell, Ed Modzelewski, Milt Plum,
Ray Renfro; those were some of the names on the
1958 roster.

Before the game, Gil Mains said, "The only thing
you don't have to worry about is the trap play. The
Browns never trap." What I should've known is that
the Browns ran ninety-percent traps. They trapped
me all afternoon. And Gil told me after the game, "I
think I should have my job back." But I played the
rest of the season as starting tackle.

We had a dismal 4–7–1 record that year. Still,
George Wilson was just wonderful to me. He
brought me along diligently, without applying much
pressure. Good games and bad, his attitude didn't
change. He kept cool—rough and gruff as he was—as
long as I gave my best. I got to love that man.

Meanwhile, my brother Teddy had finished his first
pro season with Pittsburgh. He was traded to the
Steelers shortly after George Halas of the Chicago
Bears signed him as a free agent. Halas masterminded
the deal. An illegal deal. But he got away with it.
This is how it happened: Halas thought Teddy needed
additional seasoning at the guard position, so he purchased Abe Gibron, a veteran guard, from the Philadelphia Eagles and made a handshake arrangement with
Steeler owner Art Rooney to have Teddy play in
Pittsburgh for two years, then return to Chicago *if*
the Bears wanted him. Teddy was dismayed, but there
was nothing he could do about it. He went to
Pittsburgh. Not long after that we sent Bobby Layne
there.

During a Christmas family reunion in Gary, I asked
Teddy a lot of questions about the Steelers. He

seemed depressed, unwilling to say very much about the team. When I asked him about Bobby Layne, his eyes narrowed. "I can't handle that man," he said. "Every time I turned around he yelled and screamed at me."

The scenes keep moving like color slides through a projector. A picture comes up in my mind. A picture of Johnny Unitas, quarterback of the Baltimore Colts.

It's 1959. Unitas is a four-year veteran, heading toward a league passing record of thirty-two touchdowns. Now he's on the attack against us, holding the ball at his belt, moving down the sideline, moving with deceptive speed to a sure touchdown.

It's a turning point. I wrestle away to the outside, brush past Colt fullback Alan Ameche, chase Unitas parallel to the line, and blast him off the field just before he can get in for a score. That's the picture I have of an autumn afternoon in Detroit. No big deal. We lost the game; the third in a row since the season started. But the point is, from that time on, I knew I was good. As good as any tackle in pro football.

We played the Steelers in Pittsburgh that year to a 10–10 deadlock. After the game I went into the Steelers' locker room. Bobby Layne saw me and lifted his voice above the clatter. "I'll be a sombitch if it ain't Tippy!" I mumbled something polite, then looked around for Teddy. He was sitting on a stool, expressionless. "How you doing?" I asked. All he did was crinkle his face and shrug his shoulders. Then we talked a little, and he got up, walked me to the door, and said, "I'm in over my head around here. But things will straighten out. . . ."

"Sure, Teddy, sure."

As I was going out of the stadium, a Steeler lineman came up alongside. "What's going on with Teddy?" he asked.

"Nothing, I guess. Why?"

"He keeps to himself. He doesn't say two words to anyone. Just thought I'd ask . . ."

"Aw, he's okay. Teddy gets into moods, that's all. He'll be busting out any day now."

A gang of kids surrounded the Steeler lineman, seeking his autograph. I squeezed through an opening, sprinted to the Lions' bus, got on, and fell into a seat, feeling so weak it was a strain just to lift my head.

We had another lousy year, losing eight games and finishing next to last in our division. Problems at quarterback hurt us during the season. Tobin Rote and Earl Morrall shared the position. They failed to move the offense with any consistency. Only Nick Pietrosante, a fine rookie running back from Notre Dame, showed flashes of raw power, but the offensive line creaked along on tired feet, with Lou Creekmur and Charley Ane finally retiring in the off season. Meanwhile, John Gordy developed rapidly as an offensive guard.

He played first string for us in 1957. That was his rookie season. Then he quit. He couldn't take the pressure. He said Bobby Layne was on his back all the time. Not only that, he had to play against brutes like San Francisco's Leon Nomellini and Baltimore's Art Donovan. They were monsters, he said. They chewed the hell out of him, knocked all the fun out of the game for him. So, after the championship season, Gordy went home to Tennessee, rested up, then took an assistant-coaching position at the University of Nebraska. He thought coaching at college would be fun. But it wasn't. The pressures were the same. So every Sunday he sat in front of the television set to watch the pro games. He felt awful because he wasn't out there playing.

He rejoined the Lions in 1959 and we became roommates.

One night Gordy and I were talking on the plane coming home from a defeat in San Francisco. By then we were really tight friends. The subject got around to what we would be doing in town the next evening. Monday was off. Nothing to do except sleep and then maybe get together for a couple of beers and have some fun. Gordy said that was the best thing about the game. We didn't have to spend twenty-four hours worrying about what went wrong on Sunday. There was enough time for that kind of nightmare on Tuesday, when the coaches ran the game films. That's why there's so much joy in winning, Gordy said. When we win, we can forget about it. Isn't that something, he said, that a guy would go through all that torture to win, just to forget about it.

I figured Gordy had something there.

The following winter Joanie gave birth to our first child. We named him Alex. Looking down at him the first time, thinking back through my own life, my earliest years—speeding toward my childhood days and nights of innocent dreams in an Adams Street apartment—I asked the imponderables: What sort of person will my son be? What will he aim for? What will he miss? Grasping vainly for answers, I could only hope there would be a string of endless triumphs in all his days ahead.

"He'll be a somebody, this kid of ours," I said to Joanie on that first night we had him home.

Joanie looked at me as though she had just written the Book of Revelation, and said, "He is now."

That winter we purchased our first home in Detroit, from Charley Ane. After seven seasons as a Lion, he was going back to live in his native Hawaii, no longer willing to put up with the harsh regimentation of a pro football career. He let us have the house—and all the furniture in it—for $19,500. A fantastic buy. And yet, on a $9,000 football salary, I thought there was no way to pay off the mortgage unless I continued wrestling during the off season.

Pinky George hooked me up with my old nemesis from the University of Wisconsin—Bobby Konovsky. Now he was an offensive guard with the Chicago Bears. In the summer, he would join the brand-new American Football League and become a Denver Bronco. But for now, during the off season, we were tag-team wrestling partners, working the midwestern and eastern circuits as Killer Karras and Crippler Konovsky.

Our final match took place in Hammond, Indiana, about ten miles from Gary, and twenty-odd miles from Cicero, Illinois, where Bobby grew up. I remember that his father was the police chief of Cicero, so we were able to pull in a raft of hometown rooters. However, our crowd was outnumbered by an army of hot-blooded Hispanics who hollered and clamored for two funny little ballerinas called the Crazy Castilians. One looked like a carbon copy of the other; two faces no mother in the world could love. Anyway, the promoter of the match had only one thing to say when Bobby and I got to the arena: "This is not your night."

Bobby had a mind of his own. After the referee's instructions, he turned to one of the Crazies and said, "We ain't losing tonight, guys." Back in our corner, he stuck a hand on my shoulder. "I'm starting off." This was not the way we had planned it, so I said, "You've got it wrong. Listen . . . you're not really going out there to win, are you?"

"Fucking-A right, I am."

At the bell, he flew at the first little Reggie and slapped him so hard the referee fell down. I never heard a slap like that in my life. The match ended in seconds, with the Crazies lying on top of each other, glassy-eyed and not breathing too well.

We were up at the apron, taking bows, when a pregnant woman stuck her arm up and began to tug at Bobby's trunks. He didn't know she was pregnant. Otherwise, I'm positive he wouldn't have kicked her. Suddenly, the ring's a madhouse, with people screaming and advancing like a pack of starved jackals. We had to punch our way loose. I grabbed a security cop, tucked him under my arm, and took off for the locker room.

Bobby was six feet ahead, fending off the crowd, when a gorgeous brunette in a low-cut dress and flashy earrings called out, "Bobbeee-babeeeeee!"

He looked at her. She came at him with an open penknife. The damn thing splits his leg right down to the bone—*tschk-tschk*—just like that! "We're going to get killed," I told the cop. "For Chrissake. Pull your gun." He drew the cannon, and Bobby and I ran straight out of the arena to my car. On the way to the hospital, he kept moaning, "Oh, my, look at all that blood...."

Winter. At rest. Getting up late, having eggs and coffee with Joanie, dressing the baby, going shopping; to the supermarket, to the department stores, to the corner cigar store for those imported Havanas. It's 1960. Castro is still shipping tobacco to our shores. It's winter. At play. Handball at the YMCA, basketball too, and time to catch up on television, and the movies, and with friends, and to be with Joanie as much as I can. There are so many things to do. But for me, the winter moves too slow.

Now it's April. A morning sun steals over the Indiana countryside as I swing the wheel of my red

Cadillac convertible onto a familiar roadway that leads to the Westville State Hospital, where my brother Teddy is confined with a nervous breakdown.

It happened in January, after his second season with the Pittsburgh Steelers. He came back to Gary in a deep depression. He wouldn't speak to anyone, or go out of the house for days on end. One morning I went to see him and he told me there were spies outside his door. "You're home," I said. "There are no spies around here. What the hell is the matter with you?" He laughed, a fearful laugh. Then he shut up altogether.

In January he was bundled up in a robe and blanket, then driven the twenty miles from Gary to Westville—a cold, bleak institution surrounded by a wire fence. A guard waved us through to one of the buildings. Some papers were signed inside. Then a white-capped nurse led Teddy away. He didn't say a word the whole time.

When I went to see him in February, we sat together in his room like strangers on a train. I felt helpless, unable to say or do anything to keep him from staring out the window. It was as though he had gone off into a strange world and could not move out of it again.

During a visit in March, while I struggled to make decent conversation, he suddenly raised a finger to his lips. "Don't talk too loud," he said. "They're listening. They're taping us."

Not again! I walked out of the hospital in a stupor. All the way back to Detroit I clutched the steering wheel while thoughts of Teddy raced through my mind like stray bullets. Teddy . . . how fierce he was! For a brief few years he was a king in the streets of Gary. He ruled the alleys. He dominated the Sears parking lot, and Eastside Park, and the Emerson High

football team. Teddy . . . pushing, striving, trying
like hell to be the best. He couldn't be second best.
Not him. But he was! Louie was a better athlete. And
then I came along. I took over. First in high school.
Then in college. And now in the pros. Teddy . . . I
didn't know what to do. So I cursed myself for ever
wanting to be an athlete.

A week went by. I saw him again. This time he
seemed more alert. He showed signs of coming back.
We were walking down one of the corridors to the
recreation room, and he said, "I've had these feelings
. . . some things that I couldn't own up to. I don't
know how to put it. The thing is, Al, sometimes I
don't know who I am. Isn't that weird? I mean, there
are times I can't even remember my own name."

The words crawled up my throat. "You're Teddy
Karras. You're my brother. And I'll tell you something else, you big jerk . . . *I love you.*"

Early in April the resident doc told me that Teddy
was making reasonable strides toward a full recovery.

"How much longer will it take?" I asked.

"Hard to tell. So many factors involved. But I
promise you—when he asks to go home, he'll be
ready."

It's a pleasant April morning. A day for moving
along under the sun. With my car parked outside, I
rush into the Westville recreation room and find
Teddy.

"How do you feel?"

"Much better. I'm off the sedatives."

"I know. I just saw the doc. He says it'll be okay if
we go out for a while. C'mon, let's take a ride."

We drive out of the hospital grounds to a shady
spot a few miles down the road, where we stop the
car on a stretch of grass that runs to the bank of a

clear stream. We get out, Teddy carrying a copy of the Detroit *Free Press* with him. We sit on the grass under a tree. Teddy finds the sports section and starts to read.

"What's this?" he says, thoroughly absorbed. "The Cardinals have left Chicago?"

"Yeah. They open in St. Louis this September. Pete Rozelle approved the transfer."

"Rozelle?"

"He's the new commissioner."

"When did that happen?"

"In January."

"Jeez . . . I didn't know."

A few minutes later, on the open road, Teddy turns to me and says, "It'll be nice when autumn comes around."

"Uh-huh."

"As far as I'm concerned, it's the best time of year."

"Sure is."

The sharp outlines of Westville come into sight. And Teddy says, "Don't worry. I can handle things now."

"Gee, that's great . . . real great."

"Al . . ."

"Yeah?"

"You know what?"

"What?"

"I'm ready to go home."

14. In One Ear and Out the Other

A new decade.

The Green Bay Packers started the 1960s by winning their first Western title since 1944. The biggest star on the field was Paul Hornung, who set a new season's scoring record with his running and kicking game. Behind all the Packer machinery was head coach Vince Lombardi, the tactical genius who never tolerated criticism in matters he regarded as fundamental.

In the next two years Lombardi built his team into NFL champions. His offensive guards were Jerry Kramer and Fuzzy Thurston, who convoyed Hornung and Jim Taylor around end in the patented Green Bay sweep. On defense, Bill Quinlan, Henry Jordan, Dave Hanner, and Willie Davis formed a murderous forward wall. Linebackers Bill Forester, Ray Nitschke, and Dan Currie were brutally physical on all runners who encroached on their territory. Quarterback Bart Starr developed an uncanny ability to throw the ball with pinpoint precision. In the defensive backfield, Herb Adderley and Willie Wood turned on the burners to make key interceptions on short and long passes.

Power. The Pack had it to spare. And Lombardi had a message that carried a special wallop of its own. "This is a game for madmen," he said. "In football we're all mad." He also said, "As a person, I am not well enough adjusted to accept a defeat. The trouble with me is that my ego just cannot accept a loss."

But a wiser man once said, "Although the learned have often been blind, simple men have always been aware of the enemy, which is selfishness—the egotism of nations as of individuals." Hegel said that. Naturally, he never coached in the NFL.

The point I'm really getting at is this. If Lombardi had suffered just a couple of more losses here and there, George Wilson and the Detroit Lions would have won NFL championships all three years. Yep, with a few breaks here and there for our side—ego or no ego—the world might never have known that Vince Lombardi even existed.

It beats me how things get turned around in life.

George Wilson knew he had the ingredients of a championship team when training camp opened in 1960. The veterans arrived about ten days early, all fired up with that winning feeling. Wilson kept the bandwagon rolling by extolling the virtues of our defensive strength; a ground attack in which Nick Pietrosante would be the primary runner; and ex-Cleveland Brown quarterback Jim Ninowski, who showed he could throw the ball in short, accurate bursts.

The defensive line improved with the acquisition of rookie tackle Roger Brown. At six-five, weighing 290 pounds, with shoulders wide as a door, he was like a runaway locomotive—lightning fast and just as dangerous. He gave Darris McCord, Bill Glass, and me all the help we needed in the pass rush. Sam Williams, who played for Los Angeles the previous season, was almost as big as Roger, and contributed heavily as a defensive end. There were two other new faces in camp that year, both ex-Cardinals. Carl Brettschneider teamed up with Joe Schmidt and Wayne Walker to complete the linebacking trio, and Night Train Lane filled a cornerback need, which tightened a secondary that already had top players such as Yale Lary, Dick LeBeau, and Gary Lowe.

Yet, with all the talent and high hopes, the season began in defeat and ended in futility. We lost our first three games, won three out of the next five, then beat Green Bay, Baltimore, Dallas, and Los Angeles to end the schedule and finish second in the Western Conference behind Vince Lombardi and his Packers.

Cities and stadiums.

Peculiarly, every NFL stadium crowd sets its own tempo, and has characteristics that reflect the personality of the city they live in.

To my way of thinking, Los Angeles is the ideal town. The weather is always pleasant, which tends to soothe the fans. They come out to Memorial Coliseum with suntanned faces, healthy bodies, and stunning outfits to watch the Rams perform. The team never plays. It *performs*. And when something interesting happens down on the field, such as the halftime show, the fans flash brilliant smiles and wave to their neighbors. It's all very Hollywood. So I'm hoping for a rules change that will permit the officials to start every Ram game with a movie slate board and clapper stick.

Baltimore is another story. On any given Sunday during a Colt season, if the team is in the middle of a play that might win or lose a ball game, the fans can become extremely vicious. I know of a few hard-hitting contests that have incited riots in Baltimore's Memorial Stadium. And I was in one of those games.

We were coming off a 4–5 record in 1960, and the Colts were out of the running in their quest for a third straight Western Division title. Still, they had a great team in those days—Johnny Unitas, Lenny

Moore, Gino Marchetti, Artie Donovan—all of them magnificent competitors.

Well, the Lion defensive team was sticking needles into the Colt offense, smothering their runners, choking off Johnny Unitas's passes (he was playing with a cracked vertebra), and giving our offense all the motivation it needed to go in front by five points with sixty seconds left in the game. Then Unitas threw a hummer to Lenny Moore. He made the most fantastic catch I ever saw in a professional game. Lenny flew about 25 yards in the air *horizontal* to the ground, then glided to a stop in the end zone. Poor Night Train Lane. He was covering Lenny at the corner, and had given up the chase because he thought the big Colt receiver stumbled while going for the pass. When Train saw him dancing around in the end zone with the football, his face turned chalky. I thought he had had a heart attack.

Meanwhile, one whole section of Memorial Stadium emptied. The mob swarmed on the field, picked up Lenny, and carried him around the field. Train was buried in the ensuing crush. Above the noise, a voice on the loudspeaker intoned: "This is Baltimore's finest hour. . . . Let's not spoil it now. . . . Get back in the stands. . . . Please return to your seats."

That stopped everyone except two drunks who came over to the sideline, where I was still fuming over the miraculous catch. One of them whacked my helmet. I took it off and clobbered him. He fell to his knees. The other drunk pulled a knife. I stared at the damned thing for an instant, then backed away, swinging the helmet by the straps to keep from getting stabbed. While this was going on, George Wilson ran over, screaming hysterically, *"We can still win!"* Then he went looking for the rest of his players while the knifer chased me around and around the bench. Finally, as I was about to drop from exhaustion, a bunch of cops appeared. The two drunks scattered, yelping like hyenas into the grandstand.

By now, the crowd had lessened. But hundreds were still standing three-deep along both sidelines. In the confusion, Baltimore kicked off. That's when I saw George Wilson again. He was jumping up and down behind a row of fans, trying to get through the wall of bodies. Gil Mains, Wayne Walker, and I left the bench and pulled George free. "What happened? Where are we?" he asked. He had missed the kickoff.

With six seconds remaining, Earl Morrall threw a short pass to wide receiver Jim Gibbons, who was supposed to head for the sideline. But Gibbons threaded his way past the entire Colt backfield and broke into the clear. He ran 65 yards for a touchdown! And then the gun went off.

I don't know how we got into the locker room. We had to fight off the Baltimore fans, who clawed at our uniforms, spit, cursed, and carried on like uncaged lunatics. Some of them were cops.

An hour later we were driven under police escort to Washington, where we caught a plane back to Detroit. While we were still within the Baltimore city limits, I kept my eyes trained on every rooftop, expecting to see the barrel of a gun pointed straight at my head.

Which ought to prove that Baltimore fans are the hardest people in the world to satisfy.

There's something else I remember about that 1960 season. I had been selected All-Pro tackle just before our consolation playoff game against the Cleveland Browns, so I happily strolled into general manager Andy Anderson's office one day and asked for a $3,000 raise on my next-year's contract.

Anderson was an executive from the old school. He wore stiff-collared shirts and dark conservative suits.

The aura was increased by his high-domed forehead, bald and shiny at the top; by his dark caves for eyes; by his mouth, which was thick and hard-set; by his square and pugnacious chin; and also by the way he spoke. He used his voice like a ventriloquist, throwing it in a dry, inflexible stream of words that contained little or no emotional content. Another interesting thing about Anderson. He was completely deaf in the right ear. He always sat his visitors on the left side of the room in order to hear them without straining.

And there I was, asking for my $3,000 raise.

"The Lions will be more than fair with you when we evaluate all the players next spring," he said. "But for now, I can't promise you an increase."

I got up. "Yes, sir. I understand."

Then I moved over to his right side and said, "You're a miserable prick."

He swiveled his neck around. "What's that?"

"I said the months will go quick."

"True. So very true, my boy."

I started back to his left side. "Listen, could you make it a two-thousand-dollar raise?"

"No, Alex. Not one penny more. Be patient. We'll talk about it in due time."

"Okay," I said, shuffling toward his bum ear again. Then, while he was still turned toward the right, I said, "You're a great big asshole."

"What's that?"

"I said, I don't want to create a hassle."

"Wonderful. Is there anything else?"

"No. I guess we've said it all."

In 1961 the NFL increased its playing schedule from twelve to fourteen games. So I made an appointment to see Andy Anderson again, figuring he'd go along with a $3,000 salary increase, because I'd be playing two more games that year. He listened attentively, then said the Lions couldn't afford to give me any raise at all. Economics, he said. I walked out of his office stunned.

A dozen other players received the same treatment, even though they had played inspired football in 1960. Harley Sewell, Night Train Lane, Yale Lary, and Joe Schmidt had been selected for the Pro Bowl. Nick Pietrosante broke the Lion rushing record. Jim Gibbons led the club in pass receptions. Gail Cogdill ran the most yards as a receiver. And John Gordy, Darris McCord, Wayne Walker, Bill Glass, and Ollie Spencer also felt they deserved salary boosts off their performances in 1960. To no avail. The demands went into Andy Anderson's good ear and got lost in the other.

After weeks of fruitless haggling, he decided to call us all in for an opening meeting on the issue. There was a blackboard in his office. As soon as we found places to stand or sit, he started to scribble numbers on the board:

$$\begin{array}{r} \$ \quad 1,500 \\ \$ \quad 15,000 \\ \$ \quad 65,000 \\ \$ 185,000 \end{array}$$

Etcetera.

Then he pointed to the numbers. "This is for the toilet paper you've used at Cranbrook. This is for the meals you've eaten. This is for the plane trips. This is for the hotels you've stayed at . . ." Etcetera.

Whether the figures were right or wrong, I don't know. But after we had gone through a grueling discussion for about an hour, Night Train Lane lit a cigar that smelled like burning rubber. Then, hands on knees, head down, he crossed and uncrossed his legs and said, "Oh, fuck! Oh, fuck, Mr. Anderson . . ."

Anderson took a look at Night Train, sniffed the

foul-smelling air a couple of times, and went right back to the blackboard. "This is for the laundry bills. This is for the office expenses. This is for the insurance . . ."

We were ready to leave, totally dissatisfied, feeling sick to our stomachs, when Night Train raised his hand.

"Yes, Mr. Lane?" said Anderson.

"About what you was saying . . ."

"Yes?"

"Is I under the *consumption* there ain't no more money?"

That ended the meeting.

As a footnote to this, the Detroit fans probably thought we were worth next to nothing after losing all our home games in 1961, which included a merciless 49–0 rout by San Francisco. On the road, though, we won every game but one, and that ended in a tie with the 49ers. So we finished second in the Western Division.

Meanwhile, the Packers, after losing to us on opening day, won their next six games, clinched the Western title, and went on to beat the Giants for the NFL championship.

By then, I was selling used cars for a friend of mine, a fellow named Hoot McInerney, who owned the Northland Chrysler agency. I loved talking with the customers. They were average, everyday, working people. Some of them knew I played for the Lions, and that helped fatten my commissions. I earned close to ten thousand dollars working for Hoot during the off season. Almost as much as I had made as a second-year All-Pro.

15. What the Hell's Going On Here!

Then it was back to life in the "pit."

September 16, 1962. We kicked the brains out of the Pittsburgh Steelers at Tiger Stadium. The final score was 45–7. Quarterback Milt Plum, making his debut as a Lion after five seasons in Cleveland, passed for three touchdowns. . . .

Observation: Plum's a pipe smoker. Now, there's nothing wrong with that, except that a pipe smoker spends so much time cleaning out the bowl and putting in the tobacco, he usually burns up all his energy before he can puff on the stem. So I can never figure out pipe smokers. And I certainly can't figure out Milt Plum. Look at him now. He's in the locker room after the game, puffing on his pipe and calmly telling the reporters he feels like he's just started a brand-new career. "I was more nervous out there than I've ever been in my life," he says. Then he starts to clean out his pipe again and the reporters walk away.

September 23. We smothered the San Francisco 49ers, 45–24, before fifty-one thousand fans at Tiger Stadium. In his second start as Lion quarterback, Plum passed for four touchdowns. That tied a club record.

September 30. Our first road game at Memorial Stadium in Baltimore. We beat them, 29–20. In the third quarter, Plum ripped through the Colt line on a quarterback sneak and ran 45 yards for a touchdown, which sewed up the game.

147

October 7. There was never a darker moment in Lion history. No single loss ever cost a team so much. It cost us the championship. There was absolutely no reason for it to happen. The bitterness that set in lasted for seasons to come. . . .

Observation: We're ready. Lord, are we ready for Green Bay this day! We all feel the Packers are wearing championship rings that should be ours. And when Vince Lombardi and his team take the field, we know they feel it, too.

The rain clouds open and close above Green Bay's City Stadium. We clatter down the ramp and run through the tunnel to line up before a chanting, cheering, booing crowd. An enormous cheer goes up on the last notes of the "Star-Spangled Banner." We break and go into a sideline huddle. George Wilson says, "Keep cool. Keep your eyes open and your heads screwed on. Let's go!"

Wayne Walker gives the signal. He kicks. . . . The ball is up . . . a high arch . . . Tom Moore moves back . . . takes it in the end zone . . . touches it down.

They're driving. Hornung and Taylor are picking up short yards. Starr hits Max McGee and after that Taylor pulls out of a trap and we're all chasing him and finally he's stopped on our 13. Then we draw an offside penalty and the ball moves up to the 8. Then Taylor gains a yard. And then he slips on the wet grass and loses a yard. It's third and eight. Starr rolls to his right. I lunge, miss, roll on the turf, and see the ball sail into the end zone, untouched. We've stopped them.

Lombardi calls for a field goal. Hornung kicks it from the 15. They're ahead, 3–0.

We change sides. And they can't run or pass or do anything against us. We have them bottled up on their own 30 after a holding penalty. Starr drops back, starts circling. He's in trouble. I hear the smack of shoulder pads and see Starr twisting, diving, losing the ball. I fall on it. "Christ!" yells Schmidt. "That's great! Great! We've got the mothers!" We're in possession and I'm back on the sideline, helmet off, watching our offense.

We go down the field. *Boom—boom—boom!* And then Danny Lewis sweeps into the end zone. Wayne Walker kicks the extra point to give us a 7–3 lead.

Second half. They're hurting. They're messing up: fumbling, dropping passes, hearing footsteps. Our defense is all over them—blitzing, trapping, tackling, rubbing their noses into the mud. But they get close one more time. To our 8. And we stop them again. So Hornung kicks his second 15-yarder. Our lead is cut to one point. The third quarter ends.

Nine minutes left in the game. Wayne Walker has just missed a field goal. We move out to Green Bay's 20. Joe Schmidt sets the defensive alignment. The Pack goes into a double-wing. We blitz. Too late. Starr unleashes a bullet to McGee for a first down on their 30. Then he hits Ron Kramer for 15 more yards. Then Hornung catches one up the middle and drives to our 42. "Damn!" I say. "What's going on here?" Schmidt calms me down. We dig in for another blitz. Now Starr glides to his left, in the clear and protected. He floats a high, wobbly pass downfield. McGee can't reach it. Neither can cornerback Dick LeBeau. It falls dead on the sideline. Okay. Second down. They call a quick screen, but Schmidt and Walker grab Tom Moore before he can worm into the secondary. On third and eight Roger Brown decks Taylor for no gain.

The clock's running down and Lombardi's screaming "Field goal! Field goal!" Hornung tries one from our 47. It's short. Pat Studstill gobbles it up on the 5. He plows back to the 22, going down slowly under a pile of late-hitting Packers. Plum leads our offense onto the field. Two cracks into the line and a pass get us a first down on our own 35. A run goes nowhere. Then Plum throws one away. Third and nine. Plum fades back, looks for a primary receiver. There goes Jim Gibbons down the sideline. He stretches out, leaves the ground, and makes a diving catch right in front of Lombardi. We're on their 47 with two minutes to go. Then Pietrosante picks up 5 yards with a slant into the line. Green Bay calls a time out. Plum comes running off.

"Control the ball!" says Wilson. "Don't give it up!" Plum nods, trots through the mud, and kneels for the huddle. From the sideline, I turn to Schmidt, slap his helmet, and say, "We've got the game!" He sticks out his hand, grins, then we both turn to watch our offense go to work.

A sweep to the left fails. Third and eight on the Green Bay 49. Lombardi calls another time out. There's one minute forty-five seconds left. Plum breaks the huddle. I'm expecting a run. No question about it. One more run will eat up thirty seconds. Then a punt by Yale Lary, best in the NFL, and we'll have them pinned near their own goal line. We've got them by the balls!

Hey! What the hell is Plum doing! He's in the goddamn pocket. "He's getting ready to pass!" I scream at Schmidt. And Schmidt says, "The guy is crazy!"

It happens. Flanker Terry Barr runs a post pattern, then starts his cut to the outside. His foot slips. He slides into the mud. I see the ball whizz past his head and into the cornerback's hands. Herb Adderley's got it. He's flying down the sideline and I'm hollering, "Plum! Plum! You pipe-smoking jerk!" Somebody makes a tackle. Christ, where did the sonofabitch go down? I don't know. I'm not even looking. I see Plum walk slowly off the field, his face impassive.

They're on our 18. One minute left. I'm out there now, kicking the turf, roaring at guard Jerry Kramer, "C'mon, c'mon . . . I'm gonna bust your face!" The snap. I get by Kramer, and grab Hornung and take him down. Then I nail Taylor 3 yards from scrimmage and Lombardi stops the clock. There are thirty-five seconds left. We stand with our heads down, hands on hips, waiting for a blessing. Their field-goal team comes out. I turn around. The goal posts look wide as a highway. The whistle blows us back to the line.

The snap. I rush, claw my way up a guy's shirt, over his shoulder, stretching high, but not high enough. The ball is there and then it's gone. *Poom!* The referee's arms are raised. The Packers are ahead, 9–7.

People come running past me. It's our kickoff-return team. I grab a towel on the sideline, wipe the mud from my eyes. I hear the cheers. The clock gets down to seventeen seconds. More cheers. Then four seconds. A roar.

It's over. We have just blown the most important game of our lives.

We hit the locker room and everybody is asking: "Who called that play?"

"Did you call that bullshit play?" Joe Schmidt snarls as he gets to Plum, who's peeling off his jersey.

"None of your business," answers Plum.

I pinwheel my helmet around by the straps and fire it at Plum's head. It misses by two inches and bangs against his locker door. He quivers, then sits down on his stool. Wayne Walker backs me off, but some other guys are spitting at Plum's feet and cursing him for throwing the ball. Then George Wilson jumps in and tells us to break it up. He's pushing Schmidt away at the same time, almost in tears as he does it. The press comes in. The place is a morgue. Wilson takes the blame for having called the play. But I don't believe it.

We had one more shot at Green Bay that year. On Thanksgiving Day. Before that we played six games, losing only to the Giants at Yankee Stadium. Meanwhile, Green Bay continued to win. They were undefeated in ten starts and held a two-game conference lead when the rematch started in Detroit.

On that day—in chilly, wind-biting weather—in front of the second-largest crowd ever gathered at Tiger Stadium, we proved the Pack could be beaten. We won, 26–14. But the twelve-point margin meant nothing. It wasn't that close. We blitzed, crowded, and shocked Lombardi's men from opening kickoff to the final gun. Ten times our front four and linebacking trio swept past the Packer guards and blocking backs to bring Bart Starr to the ground. He was thrown for 110 yards in losses. We decked the Packer runners seven more times for losses. Big Roger Brown led the charges with five individual sacks. The defensive rush was so brutally organized it produced nine points after only eighteen minutes of play. Following the second-quarter kickoff, Brown caught up with Starr near his own goal line and jarred the ball loose. Sam Williams snared the fumble on the 6 and ran it in for a touchdown. Three minutes later, Brown was at it again. He snaked past Packer guard Fuzzy Thurston and tackled Starr in the end zone for a safety.

Oh, how we beat them! We knocked the bejabbers out of them, that's what we did. Then we won our next two games before losing to the Giants on the last Sunday of the regular season. But the Packers went on to defeat the Rams, the 49ers, and then the Rams again, to clinch the Western championship. We settled for a Playoff Bowl game in Miami against the Steelers.

On December 30, Vince Lombardi's "Greatest Team of All Time" (I still think we were better that year) played the New York Giants at Yankee Stadium for the NFL championship. A group of Lion players gathered at Archie Stone's Miami digs to watch the game on television. A beer-and-pretzels party. Present and accounted for were Wayne Walker, John Gordy, Joe Schmidt, Gary Lowe, Sam Williams, Night Train Lane, and me.

Just before the opening kickoff, somebody said, "Hey, let's make a bet." Each of us came up with fifty dollars.

It was a great game. Green Bay led at halftime, held off the Giants late in the fourth quarter on a recovered fumble, and won by a score of 16–7.

Night Train Lane was the only one who bet on the Giants.

16. Good night, Chet . . .
Good night, David . . .
Good-bye, Alex!

All my life, even as a kid, I've known people who like to gamble. That doesn't make me unusual, because I'm Greek. If there's one trait a Greek has above all others, it must be his instinct to lay down a bet on just about anything that has odds attached to it. It's been part of our ethnic character for thousands of years.

My father, for example, had a bettor's passion for horse racing. His favorite tracks were Arlington Park, Northvale Downs, and Washington Park. Because he was always working and could never find the time to bet pari-mutuel, he'd place his bets through Sam (the Banana) Bellos, who spread the money around with every bookmaker in Gary.

It was easy to find the bookies. They used the bars and pool rooms for a hangout. At the age of twelve, I was drawn to the Fifth Avenue Pool Room, the best pool room in town. A brightly lit establishment, not far from where I lived. It became a nightly haunt, a place where I could watch the bookies pay off or collect on the races while I shot rotation or eight-ball with my neighborhood friends.

How I loved to roam around between games and look over the shoulders of older customers, who'd be playing cards, or rolling dice on green-felt tables; laughing and cursing, winning and losing nickels and dimes as though nothing else mattered in their lives. And always the sound of a ticker-tape machine clacking away in the rear office to add a touch of drama to their dull, drab lives.

Sometimes gangsters came in. They wore padded suits, sported diamond rings on fat pinkies, and froze people in their seats or in the middle of a shot until *business* was taken care of. In the pool room, under cold fluorescents, confidence and fear lived side by side.

This is what I recall of those long-ago days. So it shouldn't be a shock to anyone that, as I grew older, the gambling habit stayed with me.

I never thought it was sinful. I never attempted to hide it or felt a need to do so. For me, placing a ten-dollar bet on a horse, or a fifty-dollar bet on a ball game, represented nothing but good, clean fun. It's the best kind of fun, because it usually happens when I'm around a bunch of nice people.

Like Jimmy Butsicaris. He owned what had to be the smelliest bar of all time. It was located in the Greek section of Detroit. On a warm summer evening, with a western breeze going, beer lovers could pick up the aroma from as far away as Windsor, Ontario. Among Jimmy's clientele (which included a broad range of working-class drunks) there numbered a fair share of athletes, politicians, and newspapermen. They'd come in and slug down a few drafts, relax, and lose themselves in pleasant conversation.

In the fall of 1960, Wayne Walker told John Gordy and me about a fellow he had met, a sports nut by the name of Jimmy Butsicaris, who ran a bar called Lindell's A.C. Let's stop in one night, said Wayne. We did, and Jimmy was everything that Wayne had said about him. He was a handshaker—a guy with flair; short, stockily built, with straight black hair, a winning smile to go with a handsome face, and he wore expensive, snappy sport jackets and turtleneck shirts. His brother, John, was a full partner, and tended the bar while Jimmy, the more gregarious of the two, pulled the customers in and got the action going. Everyone hung loose and generally had a good time. The loosest people of all were the athletes. Jimmy treated them like gods. If someone at the bar spoke to them in an aggressive way, he'd make a big scene, visibly upset over what he'd consider the ultimate affront. So there'd always be a private corner waiting if a player preferred to be by himself for a while. An appealing feature for Wayne Walker, the shy type, not very comfortable around strangers and pushy fans. As for me, Lindell's proved to be a refuge, too. In the laughter and mellow buzz, there was a sense of belonging, as though I had been magically transported to my hometown and set down among relatives and friends—people I could trust and relate to. I could spend two, three hours at Jimmy's bar and leave the place feeling happy and relaxed.

That's how the trouble started in 1961. A rumor here, a *confidential* word there, reports that filtered in from undercover agents, informers, and all kinds of paid spies to the Detroit police commissioner's desk, to the local FBI, and to the ears and attention of Bill Ford and NFL commissioner Pete Rozelle. I had been observed as carefully as a bug under a microscope.

Sometime in the fall of 1961, Jimmy told me the building that housed Lindell's would shortly be demolished. He had made plans to buy a property just two blocks away, renovate it, and open up a new Lindell's. Would I be interested in becoming a partner? Of course I would. Lindell's success was largely due to Jimmy's contacts with the money people in town. And there was no doubt that my reputation as an All-Pro football player would help to make the bar an even bigger success. I pictured hundreds of Lion fans coming in on a regular basis to have a drink or two, shake my hand, and tell their friends about it down at the office the next morning. The whole idea made sense. I felt good about it.

I asked Jimmy what it would take for me to become a partner. Forty thousand would do it, he said, for a one-third share of the new Lindell's A.C. Cocktail Lounge. He gave me time to think it over. The new site first had to be gutted, architectural plans drawn up, and fixtures bought and installed before Lindell's would be ready for its reopening.

Okay. That's the background of my eventual partnership with the Butsicaris brothers in the bar business. Now, let's go over to another place, not too far from Lindell's—a really decent Greek-style restaurant, appropriately called the Grecian Gardens. It was allegedly owned by underworld people, but I never took the whispers and offhand remarks seriously. All I care about was the atmosphere and meals. No complaints there. What a menu! And an amiable Greek named Custos Colacasides, known more familiarly as Gus, fronted the restaurant. He'd always have a good table for me and made sure the service was fast and efficient. So I got into the habit of going to the Grecian Gardens about once a week, generally late at night. The action guys would also be there—gamblers, bookmakers, hustlers, maybe some of the toughest monkeys in Detroit. Well, that was their business. If they wanted to come over to my table, slap my back, strike up a conversation, fine and dandy. To me, they were just a bunch of sports fans. I liked them. They liked me. I wasn't about to be a prude.

All the while, without my knowledge, interested parties were checking out every move I made.

Shortly after Jimmy Butsicaris and I talked about a partnership arrangement, Andy Anderson summoned me to his office. He said he didn't want me to go into the bar business. I was surprised. The deal had not been discussed with anyone except my family, Wayne

Walker, John Gordy, and a couple of other close friends.

"Why not?" I responded sharply.

"I happen to know the people you want to get involved with. They're gangsters and hoodlums, guys you have to stay away from."

"The hell I will. Jimmy Butsicaris wouldn't own a license if he was that kind of character. He has a license. To my knowledge, he's never had a major violation. He's never been accused of anything, convicted of anything, and if I want to go into business with him, I stand on my rights to do so—without having to listen to a lot of wild, unfounded charges about his reputation."

Anderson tried another tack. "Look, Alex, I'm not accusing you of doing anything wrong. It's just that we don't think you should get mixed up with people who may hurt your football career."

I blew sky-high. "Listen, if Butsicaris was one of those loafers who didn't do anything except feed on innocent people, I'd stay away. But he works sixteen hours a day in that goddamn tavern. He's as honest as any man I've ever known. If I want to go out and make an honest living by becoming his partner, you know what you can do if you don't like it!"

He stood up, now equally agitated. "I can prove what I have said!"

"Yeah? Put it down on paper and sign it. I'll take it over to Jimmy, and then we'll see if he agrees with you."

"I'm not going to do that. There are others who have the facts. . . ."

"Well, until *you* can prove it, you better shut your mouth. Otherwise there'll be a lawsuit on your desk."

"Karras, I'm warning you here and now: If you go into the bar business with Jimmy Butsicaris, the Lions will take steps!"

"The only steps you can take is to trade me. And I'd appreciate it if you would."

At the door, I got in a parting shot. "And tell this to Bill Ford while you're at it. I'm only making twelve thousand dollars here. I would just as soon make thirteen thousand working behind a bar, because I need the money."

A couple of months later, Anderson sent for me again. "I'll get right to the point, Alex. We know all about your chums over at the Grecian Gardens. Stay away from there."

"It's a public place," I said. "So I intend to go right on eating there, no matter what you say."

I walked out, suppressing an urge to land a haymaker on Andy Anderson's chin.

Out one revolving door and into another. One morning the phone rang at my house. I picked up to hear someone say he was from police headquarters. Would I mind coming in to see Commissioner Edwards?

George Edwards had made a name for himself campaigning for the elimination of crime in the state of Michigan—no matter who it hurt. Every time he needed a headline he'd go to Greektown, nab a few down-and-out Greeks in a coffeeshop, and tell people the cops were cleaning up Detroit.

Now I was in his office, listening impatiently as he painted a verbal picture of Mafia history. When he got up to Al Capone, I interrupted. "Have I done anything wrong, commissioner?"

"Well, no . . ."

"Okay. Thanks for the lecture. If you find any Mafia people, put them in jail. But don't bug me. I'm leaving."

Over the winter months of 1962, and into the

spring, Anderson's warnings and police commissioner Edwards's insinuations didn't interfere with my desire to be Jimmy and John Butsicaris's partner. At Lindell's, we'd sit around and scheme up ways in which the new place could make a pile of money. Once in a while, as part of the conversation, Jimmy would say he was going to lay a bet on this basketball team or that baseball team. I'd join in and make a bet, too. In the previous months on four or five different occasions I had dug into my pocket and come up with a fifty-dollar bill to bet on the football games. I remember losing more times than I won. That was the extent of it.

A hot August evening at the bar. Tony Giacalone (a good customer) and seven or eight of his pals are going down to Cleveland in their party bus to see the Lions play the Browns in an exhibition game. I'm invited to ride back with them. John Gordy also agrees to come along.

August 18, 1962. The game is over. George Wilson has given Gordy and me permission to return to Detroit using our own transportation, instead of the team plane. We leave the ball park and board a spiffy silver and blue bus. Inside, Giacalone and his pals hold up their chilled beer cans and cheer us into our yellow, rubberized plastic seats. We pull out of the parking lot, looking through windows that are lined with yellow curtains. We play cards, drink beer, tell a few stories, and have a good time.

Behind us, the traffic is heavy going into Detroit. One car in the pack is magnetized to our tail. It belongs to the FBI.

"Okay, Alex, this is it!" said Andy Anderson in his office the next morning. "I just received a call from police commissioner Edwards. He said he talked the

FBI into trailing that bus you and Gordy took out of Cleveland yesterday. The report I get is this: On the bus were bums, racketeers, and undesirable elements who do not belong in a professional football player's life. . . . On the bus were your bar partners, who are known gamblers. . . . On the bus are the guys you eat with and drink with in Mafia-owned establishments. . . . On the bus . . ."

"We've gone around that track three times now. What else?"

"Get rid of your interest in Lindell's. That's final."

"Mr. Anderson, you can do me a real good favor. Trade me as soon as you can."

The 1962 regular season comes and goes. On December 31, the morning after Green Bay beat the New York Giants at Yankee Stadium to take the NFL title, and while the Lions are in Miami for the Playoff Bowl against the Steelers, I get a phone call from Pete Rozelle. He wants to see me at noon. "Come to my hotel . . . use the back door . . . meet me in the upper lobby. . . ."

The cloak-and-dagger routine grows more ominous. A league attorney and a stenographer are present in Rozelle's hotel room. The questions start. The names go round and round:

Butsicaris . . . Colacasides . . . Giacalone . . . Butsicaris . . . Colacasides . . . Giacalone . . .

"Did you or did you not ride on Giacalone's bus?"

"Yes, I did."

Rozelle explodes. "Who the hell do you think you are, doing a thing like that?"

"I don't want to go through the whole thing again. If you want to accuse me of doing something wrong, say it now."

"Have you ever bet on league games?"

No answer.

"How many games have you bet on, Alex?"

"I don't know . . . a few."

"Did you bet on the championship game yesterday?"

"Yeah, I bet on it."

Rozelle shakes his head. "You could be in a lot of trouble. There's an investigation going on."

We recycle, go on again. I tell him I haven't done anything to be ashamed of. I haven't thrown ball games. I haven't bet against my team. I don't have any ties with criminals. I'm telling the truth.

"Will you sign an affidavit to that?" asks Rozelle.

I agree.

A few days later, while we're getting ready to play in the Pro Bowl at Los Angeles, a reporter from the Detroit *News* calls. He wants to confirm a statement made by Andy Anderson, that he's trying to get me to sell my interest in the Lindell bar. I tell the reporter, "If the Lions try to do that, I'll fight them. I'll sue them. If they put the bar off limits, I'll quit for sure."

On January 7, 1963, the story hits every major newspaper in the country. Two days later, banner headlines cross the front page of the Detroit *News*:

RODE PARTY BUS—KARRAS
LIONS' CONTRACT RULE: SHUN GAMBLERS

The rule pops out under the headline: *Players must not enter drinking or gambling resorts or associate with gamblers or other notorious characters.*

Interestingly enough, further down in the story, Bill Ford calls the phrase " . . . a pretty vague term to throw at people. I know there is a certain gambling element that seeks out sports heroes and tries to buy them dinners. They're sports fans, too, and they are flattered to be seen in the company of these players. The whole thing has been blown out of proportion."

So began the last phase in a series of events that finally brought the full power of Pete Rozelle down on my neck. The whole hypocritical affair probably would have been reduced to an insignificant footnote in NFL history if I had not opened my mouth on one of the most important television shows of that era—the "Huntley-Brinkley Report."

A day after the Detroit *News* ran their inflammatory article about the "hoodlum-operated" bus ride from Cleveland, a Los Angeles NBC newscaster named Dave Burk called me. He wanted to know if I'd be available for an interview on David Brinkley's program. I was confused.

"Do you want me for the 'Brinkley Journal,' or the 'Huntley-Brinkley Report'?"

There was a difference. The Journal was low-keyed, relatively philosophical in content. The H-B Report, on the other hand, was far more controversial. With millions of viewers watching every night, Chet Huntley and David Brinkley delivered slick, exposé broadcasts that produced the highest Nielsen ratings in their time slot.

"I won't appear on that show," I told Burk. "Only the Journal. And only if you'll allow me to say exactly what I want to say."

"Fine. Let's set up a date for the taping."

We did the interview on January 13, the day of the Pro Bowl game. Burk asked questions for thirty minutes or so.

A sampling:

"Do you bet on games?"

"Yes, I do. I enjoy betting, even if it's for a cigar. I bet the dogs in Miami, I bet an occasional horse race. But I don't bet big money on anything."

"What about the other players?"

"Well, I don't know if they do or not, but I assume this is going on."

"Can't this lead to fixing of games or point shaving in the NFL?"

"C'mon, most athletes in this league have respect for what they're doing. There's eleven players, both defense and offense, and sure, a quarterback probably has complete control of the ball game. But so does the referee. So does your best pass receiver. So does your defensive tackle. And I never knew any of them who ever threw a game, or was involved in shaving points."

The last question: "Have you ever bet on a game in which you were playing?"

"Yes, I have."

A cold, invigorating morning at the home of my in-laws in Clinton, Iowa. The kind of weather that clears the lungs and sharpens the senses. And the phone rings. Doc Greene, a top sports columnist of the Detroit *News*, is on the line.

"Alex, you're in deep trouble. NBC's busting with a story tonight. They're going to run a tape in which you admit to betting on Lion games."

"So what, Doc? I said a lot of things. Thirty minutes' worth. Most of it is going on Brinkley's Journal."

"Who told you that? You're getting about thirty seconds on the 'Huntley-Brinkley Report.'"

"Oh my God! They've nailed me to the wall! Listen, Doc, do me a favor. Try to get to Pete Rozelle. Tell him they've edited the tape down. Tell him . . ."

"I already did. And Pete says that if you're that dumb, you should handle it yourself."

Rozelle called within the hour. He told me to fly to New York right away. He was hotter than a firecracker. I didn't care anymore. I didn't care about the Detroit Lions, the police commissioner, the way my statement came out on television, or what the hell would happen once I got to New York for a face-to-face meeting with Pete Rozelle.

I told that to Wayne Walker on the plane coming in. He was also going to be grilled because of his earlier admission that we frequented the same places and knew the same characters in Detroit's Greektown. But Wayne's problem was far less complicated than mine, so he tried to cheer me up as we cabbed into Manhattan.

"I'll tell the commissioner you didn't know what you were doing when you agreed to appear on the Brinkley show," he said. "I'll tell him you were just plain dumb."

"He already knows that."

Rozelle had instructed us to be completely secretive in our movements around town. "I don't want this meeting to be conducted in the league office," he had said. "We'll get together where we won't be bothered by cameramen and press people. When you get to New York, call me and I'll tell you where to go."

Wayne dialed league headquarters from a drugstore phone booth on Madison Avenue. Our orders were to go to the lobby of the Hilton Hotel and wait for two of Rozelle's emissaries to show up. This we did. Shortly thereafter, NFL public-relations director Jim Kensil and league treasurer Austin Gunsel arrived—then promptly sped us to the Plaza Hotel on Fifth Avenue. Wayne's session with the commissioner began immediately. As he disappeared behind the Plaza elevator doors with Kensil and Gunsel (Hansel and Gretel?), I found a lobby chair and sat down. They all looked relaxed, happy—and very rich. I let my imagination take flight, selecting a stunning woman of undetermined age to bring me out of a deep depression. She wore a full-length mink coat. A ten-carat diamond ring sparkled on her finger, and her eyes flashed more brilliantly than the ring. A dream of a woman:

I could see her approaching . . . holding out a perfumed hand, saying in a honeyed voice, "Pardon me, I couldn't help but notice you. Don't say a word. Just get up and follow me to my limousine, which is conveniently parked at the curb. And then," she whispers in my ear, "the world will be ours."

Wayne tapped me on the arm. "Are you all right? You seem to be in a daze."

"Oh—uh—I'm fine. How did it go?"

"Well, my hives are gone." He grinned. I looked at my watch. He had spent ten minutes up there. Now it was my turn.

Slumped on a sofa, barely noticing the room's decor—a mélange of burnt browns and cool greens—all I could concentrate on was Pete Rozelle, whose eyes never left my face. For me, the presence of Kensil and Gunsel seemed superfluous. Rozelle was the only one that counted. He was the power and the glory and the godhead of us all, the only man in the NFL who could crush my entire career with a single stroke of his pen. Knowing this, I suddenly felt as though a large rock had crashed at the bottom of my stomach.

Rozelle dispensed with the preliminaries. "I want you to take a lie-detector test."

I lit a cigarette. "Don't I have a right to ask a lawyer about that?"

He smiled. There's no need for a lawyer, he said. The test would be a simple one. He had to know only one thing: Did I or did I not throw ball games? If the machine indicated that I didn't throw ball games, everything would be okay.

On that basis I said I would take the test.

It's late in the afternoon. I've been sitting at a table for hours, plugged into a machine, looking through a grimy window in a second-class hotel blocks away from the Plaza. It feels weird, like I'm in a wartime movie.

"Iss ze Amerikaner force prepared to strike in ze east or ze vest? Tell us, Herr Kapitän, do you haf relatifs in Berlin?"

" . . . I shall ask this question again, Alex, and you will answer yes or no. . . . Have you ever placed a bet against your own team? . . . *No.* Did you ever accept money to throw a game? . . . *No.* To shave points? *No.* To miss tackles? *No . . . No . . . No . . . NO!*"

"Have you ever bet on a National Football League game?"

"Yes, I have."

"All right, one last question. How many?"

I think and think. There was this time in Lindell's . . . and that time in the Grecian Gardens . . . and this time in Miami . . . and at that party at whats-hisname's house . . . "I think I bet five games in my whole life."

Maybe it's eight or nine or ten or a million. I don't remember. I just want to get unhooked. Unplugged. Turned off. I need air. I'm exhausted, soaked through in sweat—and completely humiliated by Rozelle and his infernal machine.

I've put in five years with the Lions, played as hard and honestly as I could. Now, deep in a jam, scared down to my socks, I hardly acknowledge Rozelle's reassurance that everything will turn out okay.

"One thing more," he says before we leave the hotel. "Don't say a word to anybody about what went on here."

It's dark as we hit the sidewalk. Rozelle and his aides nod their good-byes. In another moment they're swallowed up in the evening rush. Shivering as if I've been dragged from an icy river, I walk to the corner and flag a taxi.

"Where to, mac?"

"Who knows? Start rolling. I'll tell you later."

For two weeks I hunted pheasant on the eastern plains of Iowa. There, in retreat, with the ground frozen like cement under deep snow, I hunted and rested. In the snow, the only sounds to be heard were the sharp crack of my rifle, wind rushing through the hollows, the squawk of birds as they flew in a solid line toward a distant nesting place. In the snows of Iowa, I remembered how it was on a winter day in Gary, Indiana, when I was four years old and saw Louie pulling Nick and Teddy along on his Flexible Flyer sled.

"Loooeeeee! I want a ride. . . ."

The ride is over. The snows of Gary have long melted. Now it's early February 1963, and muddy cartons are piled up in front of the new Lindell's A.C.

Inside, the work goes on. In less than a month, assuming the Liquor Control Commission approves a transfer of licenses, the Butsicaris brothers and I will open our doors for business. To the rear, silver and blue chairs, symbolizing the Lions' colors, are set in place. Soon a pool table will be installed. I shift the chairs around, allowing for space, visualizing the effect. "It's going to be terrific," I tell Jimmy and John Butsicaris. It will be. I can mix drinks, pour them into the proper glasses, and ring up a cash register without guesswork. Upstairs, where the offices are, I will go over the books, discuss the purchase of food and booze, arrange private parties, plan good-will events. I'm learning the bar business. And I'm liking it more each day.

Meanwhile, Pete Rozelle hasn't been in touch. Whatever he's going to do, I want him to do it soon.

Wednesday morning, April 17. From my home in Detroit, I listened to the commissioner's voice as it smashed through the phone and into my brain with bewildering impact.

"I'm afraid I have bad news for you, Alex. As stated in paragraph two of your NFL contract, which empowers me to fine and suspend any player who accepts a bribe or who bets on a game . . . I am now invoking that rule. You are hereby *suspended indefinitely. . . .*"

I heard myself shout, "Rozelle, you've sold me down the river! I'll never forgive you for this!"

It's also a day of agony for Paul Hornung, the star halfback of the Green Bay Packers. His great looks, gleaming blond hair, and body-beautiful physique had earned him the nickname Golden Boy. In 1961 he was the league's Most Valuable Player. And now, on the same day that Rozelle pulled the rug out from under my feet, Paul Hornung was given the same treatment, and for the same reasons.

Five other players were fined $2,000 each for betting on the 1962 championship game between Green Bay and New York. They were my teammates: John Gordy, Gary Lowe, Joe Schmidt, Wayne Walker, and Sam Williams. Night Train Lane was never mentioned.

The Detroit Lions' organization got hit with a mild two-count fine, totaling $4,000. According to Rozelle, George Wilson had minimized information concerning the "undesirable associations" of some of his players, and the club had allowed unauthorized persons to sit on the Detroit bench during games.

What a lousy rap on Wilson. From the beginning,

he told Rozelle all he knew about my dealings with the Butsicaris brothers. Like myself, he had been around wheeler-dealers all his life. As long as they treated him with respect, as long as they didn't try to con him or get him involved in shady schemes, he'd never cross the street to avoid them. The fact is, Wilson was friendly with Jimmy Butsicaris. He drank in his saloon, had meals with him, knew his family, and wasn't ashamed of the relationship. This is what Wilson reported to Rozelle. And the commissioner saw fit to make a case out of it.

The nerve of him to say that some people had no right to sit on Lion benches. That sort of thing had been going on for years—all around the league. Comedians and actors, politicians and priests, cops and robbers—I've seen many of them sit on team benches. I've sat next to them. Some were friends of the owner, or the general manager, or Pete Rozelle himself. And Jimmy Butsicaris happened to be a friend of George Wilson, so he joined the crowd. Big deal! There was room enough for all of us.

Not now. Not for me, anyway. An hour or so after hanging up on Rozelle, I left the house on rubbery legs, got into my car, and drove out to see Jimmy.

"I just heard the news," he said. "What are you going to do?"

"You know how I feel. I don't want to give up the bar. It's my only source of income right now. But if I stick with it, Rozelle may not let me back in the NFL."

"Al, you're an honest man. If I thought it would do any good, I'd be pounding Rozelle's desk tomorrow morning, telling him just that. But my opinion doesn't count for beans in his league. Someone else will have to get you reinstated. Meanwhile, let's open the bar. We'll make a lot of money."

"I don't know. It's a hard decision."

"Well, you have to do something."

"You're right, Jim. Maybe I'll do something else."

"Yeah? Like what?"

"Oh, they've got a pretty good semipro football team in Gary. The coach says it pays twenty bucks a week and all the steel I can eat."

17. Purgatory

My luck stayed lousy. Two days after the suspension, I became embroiled in a situation that threatened to ruin any further chance of getting back into the NFL. I can blame it on being in the right place at the wrong time.

Dick Afflis discovered early in life that he could make people cringe just by being himself. As a teen-aged football player in Indianapolis, he didn't need a number. Chest sticking out, arms dangling below the knees, slits for eyes, barber-bald, and with a voice that sounded like a boat whistle, he was the most unforgettable character in the history of Shortridge High School. Everyone who came into contact with him wanted to shrink up and disappear. His *own* teammates stayed out of his way. They were embarrassed to be around him. To take it a step further, whenever children and small dogs saw Afflis marching down the street, they'd run home and stay under the bed for hours. Shopkeepers, on the other hand, put Out to Lunch signs on their front doors and prayed he knew how to read. In spite of everything, a breed of dauntless men eventually showed up in his hometown, Lafayette, Indiana. They were college football recruiters. And Purdue University prevailed by awarding him an athletic scholarship, a generous supply of custom uniforms to fit his apelike body, and sixty-three boxes of Silly Putty to keep him amused between games.

One day Afflis fell into a pensive mood. When he came out of it, he brained the Purdue line coach with his football helmet. Then he took off for Notre Dame. Failing the literacy test, he swept south to Alabama and Miami, then veered to the Far West. After the dust had settled, he was in Reno—and liked what he saw. Saloons, bright lights, and more broads than he could count on his fingers and toes. So he settled down long enough to play football at the University of Nevada, work as a bouncer at Harold's Bar, and get married. As it turned out, Afflis got married and divorced so many times, he couldn't remember which wife got what in alimony payments.

Be that as it may, in 1951 the Green Bay Packers signed him to a pro contract. He played for them until 1954. Then he quit the sport for a pro wrestling career. From that time on, he was known to one and all as Dick the Bruiser.

So much for the biographical sketch. Now, let's get on with the reason why I thought he carried his meanness too far. Two weeks before Rozelle's decision to dump me, the Bruiser and I signed for a wrestling date. It was a reflex action on my part; a gut feeling to grab outside income while my name still meant something in the sports world. Ever since the lie-detector test, hardly a night went by that I didn't twist and turn in my bed, with the same haunting questions: Will I be able to play again? Can I hang on to the bar? What if there are no options left—nothing but a clouded future to face? What then?

The semipro team in Gary? A joke. As for the American Football League and the Canadian League, I was positive they would refrain from getting involved if Rozelle saw fit to place me on a permanent NFL blacklist. These very real fears gave way to a sweet moment when Dave Gudelsky, chairman of the Michigan Athletic Commission, called to say I had been granted a license to wrestle Dick the Bruiser at Olympia Stadium in Detroit.

Gudelsky's approval (no doubt influenced by incessant media coverage of Rozelle's gambling investigation) triggered a flood of wrestling offers from all around the country. Suddenly a dozen and more promoters wanted my body. Among them was Pinky George, who offered me a lucrative contract to wrestle that year in a series of headline matches, and a gentleman by the name of John Doyle, who wanted me to sign a one-year $40,000 contract. I told them both I'd think it over.

Now it's a Tuesday evening, some forty-eight hours after my suspension. I'm counting the house at Lindell's—counting a few familiar faces among an army of curiosity-seekers, the kind that like to slow down on highways and gawk at crash victims. Some shake their heads as if I had just died. Others mumble into their beer glasses, saying how terrible it would be not to have Alex Karras playing defensive tackle for the Lions anymore. "There'll never be another one like him!" a voice rings out. "Let's drink to that!" clamors the multitude.

And the band plays on.

And then here comes Dick the Bruiser, lumbering up to the bar with an unholy gleam in his eyes, grunting and pounding his chest like King Kong, as if some gigantic pain is tearing through every ounce of his 275-pound body. "Where's that bum, Alex Karras?" he roars.

Jimmy Butsicaris is tending bar. He points in my direction. "How're you doing, Bruiser?" I call from a side booth. Bruiser's always managed to be his own best publicity agent, so I figure he's come in to drum up some publicity for the Olympia match.

He leans back, clamps his elbows on the bar like a gunslinger, and fixes me with a contemptuous sneer. "When I get finished with you, Karras, your mouth's gonna be talkin' from your asshole."

Pretty soon he runs out of the usual profanities, so he invents some of his own. The more he curses, the more tense I get. The Lindell crowd knows this is no vaudeville act. A few of the guys shift on their stools, braced for the big blow.

Bruiser sees nothing strange in his behavior. He goes right on cursing, every now and then thumping a fist on the bar with such force that bottles fall off the shelf. Jimmy doesn't appreciate the dramatics. Once or twice he reaches over and taps Bruiser on the shoulder in order to quiet him down. Each time Bruiser whirls around and tells Jimmy to keep his mouth shut. Finally, my partner comes over to my table for a consultation. "Al," he says, "the guy's either drunk, crazy, or completely stupid. No telling what's going to happen. You'd better leave before a war starts."

Whereupon Bruiser seizes him by the shirt and delivers a left hook that barely clears his head. I jump up, push Bruiser off, and start to hustle Jimmy away.

"Call the cops!" somebody yells.

Two guys run to the back and grab pool sticks from the wall. Meanwhile, Bruiser takes another swipe at Jimmy, catching him on the chin with an elbow. "Goddamn," I holler, "this time you've gone too far, Bruiser."

In another moment we're rolling around in the sawdust. At one point the Bruiser is able to wrestle a cue stick away from one of the guys. He swings it up and down, sideways and in circles—with me underneath, trying to avoid getting hit. Now we have a genuine pier-six brawl going, with everybody howling and shrieking and climbing over each other trying to get at Dick the Bruiser.

Two cops from the First Precinct arrive. Using skills that have made him the biggest match attraction in Detroit, Bruiser tosses them away with such dexterity you'd think darts are flying across the room.

A half-dozen more cops come pouring through the door. One of them belts me from behind and breaks my glasses. Then they go to work on the Bruiser. He disappears under a mountain of uniforms. About a minute later they drag him away—manacled from top to bottom in chains and handcuffs.

The night of fun and frolic cost the Bruiser five stitches under the left eye, a night in the clink, and a $400 fine for destroying a television set and a vending machine.

Two policemen landed in the hospital, one with a torn ligament in the right elbow, the other with a compound wrist fracture. As for the twenty-odd patrons, each one had a story saved for the rocking-chair days. And five thousand guys will be saying they were in Lindell's the night Alex Karras and Dick the Bruiser fought the greatest fight of all time.

For the record, we officially squared off at the Olympia on April 27. The Bruiser pinned me with a "choke hold" after I had thrown him out of the ring a few times. I collected my money and quit the game forever.

The summer of 1963 came and began to burn off. In June the new Lindell's A.C. Cocktail Lounge opened on Cass and Michigan—so plush it made the old place look like a skid-row flophouse. We gave a party to celebrate the occasion. A few Lions came in. The majority stayed away, fearing they would be suspended if one of Rozelle's spies caught them there. I understood. I didn't blame them a bit. Still, I was thankful for John Gordy and Wayne Walker. They had the guts to come in, slide into a booth, order a drink, and say, "Here's to you, Al. We're not supposed to be here, but fuck 'em all."

August. The Lions were training at Cranbrook, a big defensive tackle by the name of Floyd Peters among the new faces. He had been traded over by the Cleveland Browns for Lion reserve halfback Kenny Webb. I remembered Peters as a fairly decent player, not an outstanding one. But Andy Anderson seemed to be thrilled with his new acquisition. "Maybe he'll turn out to be as good or better than Karras," Anderson said shortly after Peters arrived in camp.

I missed the competition; the daily workouts, the intrasquad scrimmage games, the lively bull sessions late at night, even the razzing of rookies. I remembered my own ordeal, that first season in camp when I stood on a chair in the Cranbrook dining hall and sang the Iowa fight song off-key. The veterans flung Dixie Cups at me and hissed and booed, but I hung in until the last rotten note died in my throat. I missed all that. And more. There were some moments when I felt insignificant and completely alone, as if the whole world had flashed by without noticing my existence; moments in which I harbored nothing but hatred for Pete Rozelle. I wanted to lash back, to say things that would clean my valves and maybe take away some of the hurt, if not all of it.

The chance came through newspaper interviews, such as the one I gave Bob Smith of the Chicago *Daily News*.

Smith caught up with me as I stood behind the Lindell bar, mixing drinks and smiling as though I didn't have a care in the world. The questions started immediately.

"Have you asked the NFL Players Association for support or help?"

"Who are they?" I said. "I pay fifty bucks a year to belong. That's all I know about my union."

He scratched that down in his pad, then asked about my weight, saying I looked fit but a trifle drawn.

"Well, I'm about twenty pounds under my playing weight. I've been working ninety straight nights here—six until two in the morning—but that's okay with me. Business is pretty good. I guess the scandal helped."

We went on. I talked about my dedication to the game, how I had put sixteen years of my life into football, playing in pain, taking needles, not complaining, and then waking up one day to find the league treating me as if I had murdered somebody. "You think Rozelle knows about what football means to me?" I told Smith. "You think he's concerned about what I've given? Bullshit. He's just thinking of his image."

Scratch, scratch, scratch. "What about the Lions? Have they tried to help your case?"

I shook my head, thinking how far down the tube I had slid. "What difference does it make what the Lions want to do? The hell with them. If I'm reinstated, I want to go somewhere else. Anywhere but Detroit."

Stubborn pride.

At home the next morning, I'm reading the Detroit *Free Press* and there's Smith's interview jumping out at my eyes. It's eerie. Like someone else is saying he doesn't want to play for the Lions. Hey, did I say that? Wow!

I push the paper away, go to the window to look out at suburbia. Here I'm safe, protected. In a few minutes I'll take a long walk, soak up the sun, maybe wave to a neighbor. How strange. It's a perfect day for football practice and I have absolutely nothing to do except take a walk around the block.

The phone rings. George Wilson is on the line and he's hopping mad. "For Chrissake, Al, why did you have to shoot your mouth off? I mean, telling Bob Smith you don't want to play for the Lions? What the hell are you trying to do—bury yourself? Damn it, if you want to save your football career, stop talking to newspaper guys about how much you hate Pete Rozelle and the NFL! And another thing . . ."

He's still yelling into the phone and my head is spinning. I hardly know what to think, but Wilson's making a lot of sense. Now he's calmed down to the point where I can get a word in.

"Aw, I was just sounding off, saying things to make me feel a little better, that's all. If it was up to me, I'd be in camp right now—this minute—playing my ass off for you and the team. But I'm not in charge of that operation. Bill Ford is. And Pete Rozelle is in charge of Bill Ford. You want me to crawl on my hands and knees and beg them to take me back? I'm not going to do it. Not for you, George, or anyone."

"Will you listen to me! In another few months this whole thing will blow over. The public will forget. Things will change. What I'm trying to say is you'll be off the hook. Can't you see that?"

"I'm not going to crawl . . ."

"You don't have to. Just mind your own business. Don't give Rozelle an excuse to make things worse for you than they already are."

"I don't know . . . it all seems so hopeless."

His voice softened. "You think about it. Meanwhile, if I catch anyone on the squad talking about your situation with a reporter, he's gonna get hit with something a lot bigger than my shoe."

George Wilson was true to his word. Within twenty-four hours he slapped a gag rule on every Lion player and coach. The name Alex Karras would not be bandied about with the press. An automatic fine would be imposed on anyone who broke that rule. "From now on," Wilson said in a locker room meeting, "the situation is closed."

On the practice field that day a photographer asked Floyd Peters and Mike Bundra (another candidate for my job) to pose together while holding up a jersey with my old number (71) showing. Wilson came over and chased the photographer away. Right after that an iron curtain descended between me and the team. At least, as far as the public knew.

The days dragged on. I became suspicious of everyone with a notebook or a microphone in his hand. When reporters rubbed me the wrong way, I clammed up altogether. But Pat Livingston of the Pittsburgh *Press* seemed to know when to move in and pull back on my problems. One evening in early September he stopped in at Lindell's and we talked. I remember fooling around with a fly swatter during the interview. Every now and then, *whack!* one of the little buggers bit the dust. And I'd be telling Livingston between swats how miserable I was, not being able to join my teammates for the upcoming season. "You mean all those reports about you not wanting to play for the Lions are untrue?" he asked.

"I never said those things. They got it all wrong. I'd do anything to play for the Lions. Hell, man, I'd play for them for nothing."

The next day Livingston's column started the ball rolling . . . away from oblivion.

What was real? Where did the truth begin and

end? I didn't know. All that mattered was my need to play football again. If not for the Lions, then for any other pro team that would have me. For now the sentence to purgatory had rubbed my nerves raw. Every time the phone rang I thought it was Rozelle with a last-minute reprieve. Only, it wasn't. More often than not, I'd wind up talking to a reporter from some out-of-town newspaper. I hung up on the obnoxious ones. Sometimes an ingenious fan got through after securing my unlisted phone number. Then he'd proceed to irritate me with well-meaning advice that held no practical solutions. For him, a polite silence and a whispered thank you before slamming the receiver down. Once in a while, just to be different, I'd change my voice to a high-pitched falsetto: "Who's this? What do you want? . . . No, no, no . . . this is Mrs. Farthington. You have the wrong number. Please don't call again. I'm a sick woman. My heart won't take it." *Good-bye, you schmuck!* Add to all that the times when I'd hear from the night stalkers, guys who'd amuse themselves by breathing hard into the phone and then finishing with the obligatory punchline, like "Arggghhh . . . You're dead, Karras." Unnerving moments.

I went to only one game that year. An exhibition game. I sat in the stands and stared through a dense fog. I saw uniforms and numbers sweep by, a jumble of lives roll back and forth; surging, struggling, boiling like fury while a tremendous din rattled the rafters without end. *"C'mon! Move that football! Burn 'em! Go, Lions, GO!"*

I left in the second quarter, feeling a drowsy awareness of people pointing at me as if they had just seen an extraordinary sight. Crazy! Everything seemed to move in slow motion. It was me, stumbling up the concrete steps, past the fans who rushed off to the hot-dog counters and restrooms, past the ushers, past the vendors and the security cops and the little kids who ran around in circles in the parking lot and threw dime-store footballs to each other. Past all that and into my car, where I sat for God knows how long and listened to the echoes of games that would never be played again.

Six months went by. During that time I tried to construct a life for myself which, if not pleasant, would at least be endurable. Tending bar helped. Now and then I'd get away to Iowa, where I thought about things other than football. But it always came back to football. Always.

One night, while I was sitting with Jimmy Butsicaris in Lindell's, he leaned forward in the booth, his eyes moist, his face gloomy. Finally, the words came. "Look, Al, if you decide to give up the bar, nobody is going to say you abandoned Johnny and me."

"Well, I've been worrying . . ."

"Forget it, Nothing could change the way we feel about you. But all year you've been unhappy. Sometimes I see you watching the TV games—watching the team play, rooting for them to win—and it tears me up inside. Sometimes I want to cry. Al, listen to me, you should be playing football, not doing this. Sell out, man. It's your only hope."

I lowered my head, unable to reply, afraid my answer would be the wrong one. After a while, we both slid out from the booth. Jimmy went upstairs to the office, and I walked over to the bar, where Wayne Walker was sitting.

Wayno! He has a crooner's face—dimpled and boyishly disarming. He's smiling at me with that familiar gap between his front teeth. No question, he still looks like the kid who came out of Boise, Idaho, to his first pro camp in Levis, a wrinkled T-shirt, and scruffy sneakers. Now he's the sharpest dresser on the club. Right now he's wearing a plaid jacket, wine-colored slacks, and tassled, genuine alligator loafers. But the wardrobe doesn't hide the sadness in his eyes.

I draw a beer for the both of us and we start gabbing about the waning fortunes of the 1963 Lions. The team's lost five of nine games so far, and key players are on the sideline with serious injuries.

Flanker Pat Studstill is out with a knee operation. Three starting defensive backs have been crippled. Yale Lary has an Achilles'-heel injury, Night Train Lane has damaged knees, and Gary Lowe is on the shelf with a sheared tendon. Meanwhile, defensive end Darris McCord is playing below par, and two of the Lions' three starting linebackers—Carl Brettschneider and Joe Schmidt—are also hurting. Schmidt's the latest casualty. In a game against the Baltimore Colts, somebody parachuted on his head and separated his right shoulder. This leaves Walker as the only first-string linebacker healthy enough to play. Well, not quite. He has a pulled hamstring. It's been bothering him for a month. But he'll be on the field this Sunday when the Rams come in to play us.

"Remember the time we played them out on the Coast in our rookie year?" Walker asks.

"Yeah . . . I remember."

"My second start and my first interception. Had a swollen ankle then."

Yeah. Six years have passed since that day in Los Angeles. A typical California day, with the sun glinting off Ram helmets and Wayne Walker peeling back to get in front of a Billy Wade pass. Sure, I remember.

"He threw the ball right at me," Walker says. "Right in the chest. I ran thirty-five yards for a

touchdown. Damn, what a feeling. My first interception—with hightop shoes and a bad ankle."

"I know. I was there."

"Not when I hurt the ankle," Walker corrects me.
"It happened the day before—at Hollywood High."

He's told the story a dozen times. But I want to
hear it again; to satisfy a craving, a need for laughter
between friends. "What happened?" I ask.

"Well . . . we were practicing at Hollywood High
for the game, and I went over early with Tobin Rote,
Jim Martin, Bob Long, Charley Ane, Gerry Perry,
and some other guys. I was the only rookie. Anyway,
we get to the field and the gate's locked. So Tobin
Rote says, 'Hey, Walker, you climb over the fence
and get the caretaker to let us in.' That's good enough
for me, because I felt very nervous being around all
these great athletes. So I say, '*Yes, sir!*' and climb the
fence. There must have been a hundred people
watching as I go up like a frightened monkey. I
remember I had on these blue shorts, and I get to the
top—feeling absolutely terrific—and wave to the
crowd. It's my greatest triumph so far in the NFL.
Then I jumped down. And my goddamn shorts hook
on the fence. They just ripped off me and hung
on top. I couldn't believe it. There I was, in my T-
shirt, my football shoes . . . and my *jock!* Christ, I
didn't know what to do. So I ran under the grandstand."

"I should think so."

"Well, they finally throw the gate open, and
Charley Ane comes over. He throws me a pair of
shorts and says, 'Okay, boy, you can come out now.'
Then he says, 'Oh, by the way . . . somebody wants
to talk to you.' 'Who's that?' I ask. 'Goddamnedest
thing,' says Charley, 'the guy says he's a Hollywood
talent scout. He says he wants to sign your balls to a
long-term contract.' "

We let out a collective roar. Our bodies heave with laughter. But it's all part of the act. In another minute the mood changes. Now, standing behind the bar, hearing but not listening while Walker tells me how he had to soak his ankle in a tub all night to get the swelling down so he could play against the Rams the next afternoon, I recall another distant scene. The thought is drawn like a wave from the sea; clean and sparkling. Through the swirl I see us strolling along Sunset Boulevard and hear Walker shout: "Gosh, Al, isn't it fantastic? I mean, man, we're really here! Who'd ever think . . ."

Snatches of phrases. Floating sounds. Exclamations that rise and crest, then bubble away to the cold darkness. *"Who'd ever think . . . Some days I wake up laughing, actually laughing. . . . To me, this is the greatest thing in the world. . . . Hey, there's Schwab's Drugstore. Let's have a banana split. . . . Isn't that Milton Berle? . . . Listen, the coach keeps saying 'ego.' What's that? . . . Ends blocking down and guards pulling out? I never knew. . . . You know what, Karras, we're going to murder the Rams. . . . I've got the confidence. . . ."*

" . . . I'd better get on home for dinner," Walker is saying, cutting through tons of darkness. A moment later he's gone, and I'm standing there behind the bar, wiping beer glasses and wondering why so many happy thoughts of the past are wired to pain.

18. Life in a Bubble

From Prohibition days onward, Detroit mobsters have been a powerful group within the national syndicate of organized crime. They infiltrated the big trade unions and siphoned off vast fortunes from pension funds and insurance plans in order to set up legitimate businesses all over the state of Michigan. Night clubs and restaurants headed the list. I guess the mob guys picked them because they liked to go in wearing fancy clothes and have the headwaiter say, "Good evening, sir, here's your private table." Anyway, it gave them an opportunity to do business in the open—among the swells—without fear of being raided by the vice squad or other law-enforcement agencies. But just in case, they further protected themselves by hiring top criminal lawyers to provide a strong legal defense if and when federal, state, or city prosecutors felt that sufficient evidence had been accumulated to bring them before a grand jury for indictment.

Among the Mafia's battery of lawyers was Joe Louisell. God rest his soul, he was a large, heavyset man with a rich, buttery voice. But that's neither here nor there. The important thing is that during the postwar years and into the 1960s, Louisell conducted brilliant courtroom strategies that brought acquittals or reduced sentences for many underworld figures. So he gained their respect, and was permitted an occasional glimpse into their secret society. Thus, he came to know the Detroit gambling scene inside out.

Louisell was a heavy drinker. He loved to get drunk and have a good time in livewire bars like Lindell's. He'd spend two or three nights at my place, boozing it up with the crowd, charming everyone by telling humorous stories that had little or nothing to do with the professional side of his life. He'd rather talk about good food and good bourbon and pretty women and championship fights and Lion football games. Almost everything he said made us laugh. I was delighted to be around the guy. I liked him tremendously. He showed a lot of class.

One night while I was tending bar with John Butsicaris, ringing up the cash register and all that, Louisell walked in. He ordered a triple shot of bourbon and beckoned me to one of the empty tables. We sat and traded wisecracks for a while. Then Louisell began to speak philosophically about the state of the world, saying that most of our cherished institutions were controlled by hypocrites. "Since the beginning of civilization the hypocrites have been sitting on their royal asses—hatching cruel plots to suppress the underdog. They're still with us. And they're getting crueler each day."

I shrugged. "Maybe fifty years from now things will be better. Who knows? I won't be around to see it."

He gave me a compassionate nod, then swallowed his shot of bourbon. "Look, without the details, I want to make you aware of the fact that I've thoroughly checked out your bar activities. To put it into simple words, Al, you're as clean as snow."

"Tell that to Rozelle. He's one of those hypocrites you're talking about."

"I intend to. Give me an okay and I'll be your attorney."

I looked around as if he had been talking to someone else. "C'mon, Joe. I don't have that kind of money."

"Forget the money. I'll represent you for no fee at all."

"You must be kidding. For what reason?"

Point-blank, he said, "Because you deserve to be back playing football for the Lions."

Five minutes later we shook hands on the deal and he was saying, "Just go about your business and leave Rozelle to me." After that it was all laughs and stories and maybe three or four more triple shots of bourbon for Louisell. Then I went behind the bar, afraid to let myself feel too jubilant while he was still saying good-bye to some of the remaining customers. After he left, I slapped the counter and shouted, "Okay, you guys! Drink up! This one's on me!"

In early January 1964, I sat with Louisell in his downtown Detroit office. He poured himself a shot and stared glumly at the bottle. "I ran out of Jack Daniel's," he said. "Well, here goes nothing. . . ." I gazed out the window while he slugged it down.

"All right," he wheezed. "Let's get into the reason why I asked you to come down here. Dan Leonard of the Liquor Control Board called this morning."

I raised an eyebrow. "Good news or bad?"

"The best. He confirmed something that is essential to our argument for reinstatement. The liquor law in this town says that a man with his name on a license can't sell his place for a year. And after that he can't get back in the business for three more years. So here's what we have. On one hand, Rozelle wants you to give up Lindell's before he'll even begin to consider an appeal for reinstatement. But on the other hand, if you *do* get out, and Rozelle decides to permanently ban you from playing in the NFL, you may wind up playing with yourself for the next three years."

"Joe, this may seem kinda silly, but there's got to be a better way for me to spend my time."

"Exactly."

"So what do you suggest?"

"Be patient, my boy. When the NFL meetings start later this month in Miami, your formal appeal will be there for Rozelle's consideration. And we should have a decision shortly after that."

"Do you honestly believe it'll be favorable?"

"Absolutely. And I'll tell you why. Here, read this. . . ." He reached into the top drawer of his desk and pulled out a small wooden plaque. In black gothic letters, it read: DON'T FUCK AROUND WITH THE LAW.

We had a good laugh. Then he turned serious. "I believe *that*!" he said. "And deep inside, Rozelle must believe it, too. So he'll do the right thing. That's all there is to it. Simple as that." I accepted his appraisal. But Louisell added: "Do you know what you should be doing between now and February?"

"Work the bar, I guess."

"No," he said grimly. "This is important. You should go back to Iowa and forget about all this until I call you."

The next morning I left for Clinton.

It was like living in a bubble.

And outside the flimsy shell, far away and unseen— but heard about later—dark skirmishes went on between those who wished me well and those who didn't.

In late January, at the NFL meetings in Miami, Rozelle glibly said he still hadn't made up his mind. He said I'd have to wait until late February for his answer. He told that to Joe Louisell. He told that to George Wilson, too. And Wilson told the press that

Rozelle was a tough commissioner who could be the sportsman of the year if he'd let me play again. It would be a popular move, Wilson said.

Meanwhile, I played handball and basketball in Clinton, and hunted, and walked in the snow, and ran the car along muddy roads leading to tiny villages where old men sat in general stores and stared into potbellied stoves and watched the fires die. And there was a moment of timeless suspension when the Iowa land became petrified and all movement seemed to flow inside the bubble at great speed. It was as if all life existed there, passing around and through me, speeding along in an endless rush, toward an infinitesimal dot that held the pure secret to all life and all meaning. Where was it?

Louisell called one morning in early March to say we would be going to New York in a few days to meet Rozelle.

The time was at hand. And yet we sat and waited close to an hour in the reception area of NFL headquarters while the commissioner busied himself with other matters. "What kind of cat-and-mouse game is that guy playing?" I said to Louisell at one point.

"These things happen," he said.

"All the same, it isn't fair. You know what? I feel like leaving."

"I know. But you won't."

A secretary came out to get us. We walked into the commissioner's office. He sat in an executive chair behind an executive desk: a blue-eyed, dark-haired man with an everlasting tan on his executive-looking face. He wasn't smiling. There were no apologies. Just two jerky handshakes and a long pause while he looked across his desk at the two of us. Louisell started to speak when Rozelle's phone rang.

"Excuse me," he said. Then he leaned back, with a phone cradled between his shoulder and chin, a manila folder in his hands, feet up on the desk. "Yes . . . No . . . I'll look into it. . . . Of course . . . of course . . ."

"Put the phone down!" Louisell yelled.

Rozelle got rid of the folder. He smothered the receiver and said, "This happens to be important."

"This man's *life* is important," Louisell said, pointing to me.

The commissioner placed the receiver on its hook, folded his hands, and said, "All right, Mr. Louisell. I'm listening."

"What I have to say won't take long. You have unjustifiably punished Alex Karras for one year. And now I advise you to make a decision as to what he will be doing for the rest of his life. I want that decision to be made within a week. And if it's a negative decision, I will tear the NFL apart!"

That was it. We walked out, leaving Rozelle sitting there with his mouth open.

March 16, 1964. It went like this:

THE NATIONAL FOOTBALL LEAGUE
Statement of Commissioner Pete Rozelle

The suspensions of Paul Hornung of the Green Bay Packers and Alex Karras of the Detroit Lions have been reviewed separately and both players are reinstated, effective immediately.

They were suspended indefinitely last April 17th for specific violations, principally betting, of the player contract, the Constitution and By-Laws and National Football League policy.

Hornung and Karras had placed bets on their own teams to win or on other National Football League games. There was no evidence that either ever bet against his own team or performed less than his best in any football game. Further, there was nothing in the record of the cases to reflect on their competitive excellence or their intense pride in winning.

Personal discussions with Hornung and Karras have established to the satisfaction of the Commissioner that each now has a clear understanding of the seriousness of the offenses and of the circumstances that brought them about.

Therefore, taking into prime consideration the extent of their violations and also their conduct during the period of suspension, it is felt that the interests of the League will be best served by termination of the suspensions.

19. The Wolves Are Still Howling

On January 10, 1964, William Clay Ford took over sole ownership of the Detroit Lions. A large syndicate of stockholders sold him the franchise for $6 million. In cash. He could afford it. His grandfather was Henry Ford, founder of the Ford Motor Company. In a pinch, Bill could also borrow a few bucks from his wife, the former Martha Firestone, heiress to a rubber-tire fortune.

I met with him in late March, and he seemed genuinely pleased to have me back in harness. "Let's see what we can do about your salary needs," he said before the session ended. The next day I sat down and negotiated a contract with Russ Thomas, who was hired as personnel director shortly after Ford bought the club. I didn't get exactly what I wanted. But a two-year pact calling for $25,000 a year made me one of the highest-paid linemen in the game. So I was happy, and grateful to Bill Ford.

Still, I didn't kid myself. Like his grandfather before him, Bill Ford did what he had to do to get the most out of a production line. That's how the world turns, I guess.

In the summer I went back to Cranbrook. The camp still throbbed with struggle and contentment. Nothing was different. And yet the sameness had me afraid. I thought I would wake up to discover it had

193

all been a cruel illusion, an enchanting lie. Instead, a full-throated welcome brought me happily back to earth.

George Wilson was overjoyed. The first day in camp he told me just how much I meant to the over-all play of the club. "As we went along last year, I realized you were almost *impossible* to replace," he said.

And Les Bingaman, the defensive line coach, said he would be able to sleep better knowing I'd be back on the job again. And the players told me in somewhat different ways how much they appreciated my release from purgatory.

During our first intrasquad scrimmage, John Gordy raged each time we tangled on the line. "C'mon, c'mon!" he'd yell. "You gotta do better than that! You're lousy, Karras. You're nothing but a lousy mothering lard-ass!" We had a fistfight before it was over. Then we walked off the field arm in arm, our eyes all watered up with the joy of being together—of being part of something unexplainably wonderful.

Most afternoons before the evening meal, Gordy and I and Wayne Walker and Joe Schmidt and Sammy Williams and a few other guys would take off in our cars and drive a few miles along Route 22 to one of the bars, where we'd order cool drinks, listen to the jukebox, play poker, tell funny stories about former football days, and laughingly speculate about the ones yet to come. Such stories! The harder we laughed, the better I felt. In the laughter, more than anything else, I knew the guys cared about me.

The exhibition season opened and closed. I played nearly every minute on defense, and the fans' reception was great. They stood and cheered as I trotted on the field during the lineup announcements. No matter where we were playing, they hollered like a New Year's Eve crowd in Times Square every time I stopped a quarterback or a runner with an open tackle. They fired me up and I was drawn to them as never before.

The regular season started with a win over San Francisco. Then we tied the Rams. Then we lost to Green Bay, but came back to beat the Giants and Bears. After that we flew to Minnesota and played the Vikings. I remember tackling Fran Tarkenton for a 16-yard loss a minute before the game ended, which insured our fourth victory in six games.

The Baltimore Colts were next in line. An impressive win over them at Tiger Stadium would have set the tone for an unstoppable drive to the Western title. But we goofed. The Colts shut us out, 34–0.

One of their touchdowns came on a Johnny Unitas hand-off to Lenny Moore, who squeezed through a trap and galloped untouched into the end zone. Baltimore used those traps all afternoon, busting our line open just wide enough to break plays for good yardage. With my bad eyesight, the only thing I could do was sense the flow of traffic; feel my way to the runner by nerve ends—like a blind man moving around with a cane. Most of the time it helped, because all the faking and spinning by Moore was supposed to fool someone who could *see*. I used a unique sort of braille system to get at him. The slightest touch and I jumped like a cat. But the system failed when Colt guard Jim Parker submarined me on an inside trap. My left foot was stuck in the grass at the time. I had just started to pull it out when he emerged from the deep, punching up into my groin. The worst pain ever felt by a human being went through me like two balls of fire. *Whack-whack!* I actually heard the groin muscles snap. I pitched forward, then slowly rolled over on my back and blinked up at the sky. It was chartreuse!

Lion trainer Millard Kelley came barreling out to

administer first aid. "Try to straighten your legs," he said.

"If I do, Kelley, my head is going to fly into the fucking bleachers!"

A minute later he helped me to my feet and said, "Let's go! Save it for next week."

"Like hell! As long as I'm standing, I'm going to play. . . ." Kelley dog-trotted to the sideline, shaking his head in amazement. And I joined the defensive huddle with one hand under my crotch, the other holding on to someone's shoulder for support.

In the locker room, Kelley and team physician Richard Thompson eased me onto a table. "You're hemorrhaging," said the doc. There were ugly discolorations on both sides of the groin. The pain had become almost unbearable. So Thompson pumped six shots of Novacain into me. I felt like a pin cushion.

The therapy went on all season. Massages, heat, whirlpool baths, pills, shots, and more shots. Every day. They'd usually give me a shot before practice and I'd be relatively free of pain for about twelve hours—long enough to have ripped the injury some more and for the pain to get worse at night. I didn't sleep eighteen hours in a whole week for weeks. But I continued to play. My God, I'd think, I've got to make All-Pro again. I've got to prove I'm as good as I ever was. . . . Meanwhile, the Lions kept the injury a secret, the premise being that the other teams would still maintain a healthy respect for my pass rush. That's exactly what happened.

Two weeks after the Baltimore game, we took on the Packers at Green Bay. They beat us, 30–7. They outhit, outgained, and outplayed us for fifty-nine minutes. We finally got on the scoreboard when Milt Plum connected with Gail Cogdill for a touchdown ten seconds before time ran out. It was the kind of win that permitted Lombardi to use a number of reserves during the second half, including a rookie guard named John McDowell. I think I played opposite him in two or three series. In a postgame interview with one of the reporters, he said I had been real easy to handle. He said: "I guess Karras has slowed down a lot."

I read about it the next day. And it stuck in my craw.

On Thanksgiving Day we played the Bears at home. I went up against guard Jim Cadile. He not only stopped me again and again, he literally beat the crap out of me. There was only one small consolation. I managed to get past him on one play and tackle quarterback Rudy Bukich in the backfield. Cadile gave me an "I'll get you later" look and then beat up on me some more. Meanwhile, the entire Lion defense wasn't doing too well, either. Late in the fourth quarter, we lost the ball on a Bennie McRae interception. Then Roger LeClerc kicked a field goal and the game ended with us on the short end of a 27–24 score.

Now I'm facing Chicago *American* sports reporter Brent Musberger in the locker room. He flipped open his notebook and baited me with a question he had every right to ask, but not the way in which it was posed. It alluded to an opinion I had expressed about Cadile in a magazine article. Something to the effect that he was overrated as a pass defender.

"Do you think Cadile did a better job *this time?*" singsonged Musberger, flashing a supercilious smile for a big finish.

He had no knowledge of my groin injury. If he had, and then went on to write that Alex Karras was a detriment to the Lions by playing injured, I certainly would have respected his opinion. However, on that day Musberger wasn't even a decent press-box observer—the kind of reporter who generally asks: *Why did you shift right instead of left on such-and-such play? ... What prevented the pass rush? ... What caused the breakdown? ... When did the tide turn?* Questions like that. I had heard them a thousand times over in every locker room along the NFL trail. And answered most of them honestly. But on this day Musberger decided to be a wise-ass. So I ignored the question.

He repeated it again. "Do you think Cadile did a better job...?"

I exploded: "What the hell do you want me to say? You want me to say that Cadile is the greatest guard who ever lived?"

Musberger backed off, flustered. That got me even madder. I stuck a finger under his nose. "Do you want me to shove your head through the wall?"

He closed his notebook and padded away.

The 1964 season ended for us with a hometown win over the 49ers on December 13. I remember Jim Gibbons, my old Iowa teammate, flying down the field on a 64-yard touchdown pass from Milt Plum shortly after the opening kickoff, and Tom Watkins taking a 49er punt and racing 68 yards for a touchdown, and Gibbons going 82 more yards on the longest reception of his career to complete our scoring. I remember that, and the mixed cheers and boos that came down from the stands as the Lions walked off, feeling more frustrated than the crowd. Not only because we had finished in fourth place. Hell no. There were personal reasons, too, that had stripped away our pride and turned a potentially super football team into a band of malcontents.

Me included. Although nine months had passed since Rozelle lifted my suspension, I was still told where to go, what to do, and whom to associate with and stay away from. And yet, nowhere in the NFL Players Contract did it say that the commissioner or the ball club had a right to interfere with my private life. Nowhere did it say I was a machine. So I didn't act like one. I continued seeing Jimmy and John Butsicaris socially. I retained my interest in Lindell's. And through Joe Louisell, I advised Bill Ford and Rozelle what they could do if the issue were to be dredged up again.

Another thing. One of our assistant coaches tried to knife George Wilson in the back. He wanted his job. All season he whispered in Bill Ford's ear, saying George had been bad for the team, that he didn't make the right trades, select the proper draft choices, play his most able men, maintain discipline, and so forth. The whisperings were a litany of deceits waged against a great coach—a fearless, irreproachable man who lived by the golden rule every day of his life. Nonetheless, Bill Ford listened to the aide. And by degrees, he whittled down George's authority. Earlier that year, Ford gave him a free hand to make trades. Then he stepped in and turned the job over to Russ Thomas. It hurt George plenty. But it didn't affect his actions on or off the field.

The seeds of destruction were further strewn when that assistant coach spoke openly to the players about George's alleged failings. "He doesn't know how to motivate you guys," he'd say. "You'd be champions if I had charge of this outfit." His treachery turned most of us off. But a few thought he made sense, including another assistant coach. As a result, the Lion ranks were split into two camps. We lived in turmoil. And everyone felt disgusted with the situation. All the while, George Wilson concentrated on football, seemingly unaware of the intrigues that disrupted us and helped to destroy whatever chance we had for a championship.

In early December, the night before we played the Colts in Baltimore, I went to his hotel and found him there with the entire coaching staff. They were running game films, scribbling X's and O's in their playbooks—the whole bit. George got up to see what I wanted. "It's private," I said. "Can I talk to you for a minute?"

"Sure." We stepped out to the hall.

"George, I don't want to be a squealer, but I like you so much . . . and respect you. . . ."

"What's the matter, Al?"

"Well, a couple of guys in your room can't be trusted. They're looking to shaft you."

He took a deep breath, then slowly let it out. "Anything else you care to tell me?"

"Isn't that enough?"

"I guess so. Anyway, don't bust a gut over it. If that's what they want to do, let them go ahead and try."

There would be no groping, no acrimony, no hatred. He went back to his room at peace with himself, believing that he had already measured up to a fulfilled life.

A week before Christmas, Bill Ford called him in for a meeting, saying that three of his five assistants would have to be fired.

"Which three?"

"Don Doll, Les Bingaman, and Bob Nussbaumer."

George's face reddened with anger. He protested. But Ford said it would have to be that way if he wanted to stay on as head coach. Survival was the name of the game, just then. So George agreed. And the next day, at lunch, he informed the aides that they were no longer members of the ball club.

There was another meeting with Ford. General

manager Andy Anderson also sat in. He said, "We've decided to wipe the slate clean. You'll have to get rid of Aldo Forte and Sonny Grandelius."

Once more, George bent to front-office demands. Then Ford untightened the screws. "Look, Wil, it's not the end of the world. I'm sure there are five other fellows out there who can do a good job for us next year. You pick the ones you want. You're the boss. Okay?"

George nodded, fighting off an impulse to tell Ford and Anderson to take a jump in the lake.

He walked out of the office and drove away in the company's powder-blue Thunderbird to his beautiful home in Dearborn. But the wolves were still howling in his ears as he pulled up to the driveway, parked, and carried into the house an armful of Christmas presents for his wife and five children.

The next morning, over breakfast, George read his favorite newspaper. One of the columnists reported that Forte and Grandelius had already been written off by Lion management, and went on to say that a list of new candidates would be presented for George Wilson's consideration. If he refused to go along, and quit, steps had already been taken to name someone else as the new head coach.

So George Wilson quit.

Bill Ford said, "I'm surprised and disappointed."

Andy Anderson told the press, "If you want to know why he left, ask him."

Aldo Forte, his number-one assistant, said, "I feel sorry for George. He's fifty-one years old, and I don't know if he has another job."

All the other coaches expressed their regrets, too. So did most of the players.

I called him the day after his resignation. He

seemed happy. "Have a good year," he said. "Do well.
And let's keep in touch."

"Sure, George. Merry Christmas."

20. There's No Place Like Home

In 1965 seven men were enshrined in the Pro Football Hall of Fame: Bob Waterfield, Dan Fortmann, Sid Luckman, Paddy Driscoll, Guy Chamberlin, Steve Van Buren, and Otto Graham.

My mother also made it. At special ceremonies in Canton, Ohio, on May 9, Emmiline Karras Schofield was honored by the Hall of Fame as Mother of the Year. Surrounded by three of her five sons, and daughter, and her second husband—retired air-force colonel Edwin J. Schofield—she proudly accepted a plaque commemorating the occasion. As I stood behind her, gazing out at the crowd of newspaper, radio, and television people, I felt a sharp ache of regret, remembering a woman who had worked so hard during the early days of my childhood to make things just a little easier for me. I remembered her courage, the countless humiliations she had to go through because of my intransigent ways. And I suddenly recalled the look on her face—something close to fear—when I followed my brothers into a world that relied on brute strength for its very existence. At that moment it struck me that mom would have been happier if I had gone into another profession. But the years had flown, and there we were, on a May morning in Canton with official pictures being taken, and the road back to Gary seemed farther away than ever.

Then mom placed her arms first around Louie, then Teddy and me, and said, "Isn't this remarkable? I'm so excited!"

"We're all proud of you," I said in a choked voice.

"You should be. I'm the only Karras in the bunch who's made the Hall of Fame."

On a muggy September morning of that year, Teddy checked into the Cranbrook camp to meet his new teammates. He had become a Lion in typical fashion. The hard way.

The Chicago Bears had traded him to the Washington Redskins the week before. George Halas chopped him from the squad without warning, after Teddy had played first-string guard five years for the Bears. He was thirty-one, married, with a nine-month-old baby—and one on the way—and he had just purchased a new house in Gary. "I won't play in Washington," he told me on the phone the morning Halas announced the trade. "I want to be sent to Detroit. Otherwise, I'm retiring."

"Why Detroit?" I asked, waiting for him to say what I wanted to hear.

"Because it's only a couple of hundred miles from Gary, you knucklehead."

"Oh."

"Besides . . . we'll be together again . . . on the same team. Just like the old days at Emerson High."

"Teddy, do me a favor. Retire."

We laughed. Uproariously.

A few days later he came over with quarterback George Izo in a trade that sent All-League guard Darrell Dess to the Redskins, and he did well enough to make the starting lineup one month into the season. For an added thrill, we got along famously. I suppose being the only active brother combination in pro football had something to do with it, but a more satisfying reason is that we had finally become such close friends. When the season ended, Harry Gilmer—George Wilson's replacement—traded Teddy to the Rams. He played for them one year. Then he retired.

Good old Teddy. In his nine-year pro career, he enjoyed a number of solid, tangible triumphs to go along with the inevitable defeats. And, most certainly, there was never a dull moment while he played for Detroit.

How could it be otherwise? Joe Don Looney was with us.

The day Looney arrived at Cranbrook, he was curled over backward with 200 pounds of weights and dumbbells across his shoulders, and more weights attached to his neck, wrists, and ankles.

"Who's that?" rookie tackle Jerry Rush wanted to know.

"Looney," I said.

"I *see* what you mean. But what's his name?"

"*Joe Don* Looney. He played for the Colts last year."

A good-looking kid with a nice smile and a magnificent body, Looney had a terrible reputation. At the University of Oklahoma, he had slugged one of the student assistant coaches, and was suspended. Then he scandalized the whole state by calling head coach Bud Wilkinson a bigot.

Despite all the furor, the New York Giants selected him in the first round of the 1964 draft, saying he had "all the tools for greatness." At a big 230 pounds, blessed with tremendous speed, he could also punt the ball a mile. The only problem: Giant coach Allie Sherman couldn't get him out of his room to practice. So Looney was shipped off to Baltimore.

He ran the ball only twenty-three times for the Colts. It didn't bother him that much. He preferred to sit on tombstones in some of Baltimore's finest cemeteries. Naturally, it bothered the club a great deal. In the off season, head coach Don Shula contacted NFL teams hither and yon in order to dump the rather eccentric halfback. The Lions obliged by giving up linebacker Dennis Gaubetz in trade. And shortly after summer camp opened in 1965, here came Looney—dumbbells and all.

The older players wondered whether Harry Gilmer had made the right move. But Gilmer was sure he had. "I don't expect to have any problems with him," he announced. Well, during those first days in camp, Looney behaved like a perfect gentleman. And the Detroit publicity department predicted he would be the finest Lion running back since the glory days of Doak Walker in the early 1950s. But then he went on to do some truly ridiculous things that summer and into the regular season.

There was the infamous helmet incident, for example. He damaged his helmet during one of our early practices. Equipment manager Friday Macklem tried to repair it, but didn't have any success. So the next morning Looney told Gilmer he wasn't going to wear a helmet on the field.

"We'll give you a new one," said Gilmer. "You have to wear one, y'heah? It's in the rules."

"Rules or no rules," pouted Looney, "I'm not going to wear a helmet until I get mine fixed."

Now Gilmer goes over to John North, our offensive coach, and says, "John, you'll never believe this. Joe Don says he won't wear a helmet. What are we going to do about it?"

"Beats me," says North. "Why don't you ask Sammy Baugh?"

With that, Gilmer spits out a plug of tobacco, turns to Slingin' Sam, our backfield coach, and says, "I've got a problem." Then he repeats what he had just told North. Sammy scratched his chin for a second or two.

"Well, Harry, I reckon it's gonna be kinda rough on the boy, because the team's gonna scrimmage today."

Can anyone who's ever been in the game imagine this going on among coaches? I mean, if a poll of every player were to be taken, nobody'd believe such a conversation ever took place. But it did.

We scrimmaged that afternoon. Looney stood on the sideline, bareheaded, watching it all while Gilmer muttered under his breath and tried to avoid the stares of his veterans, who were amazed that he hadn't slapped Looney with a heavy fine, or, better still, run him out of camp and not let him come back until he apologized. That's what George Wilson would've done.

But Wilson was gone. And we were "saddled" with Gilmer, a former University of Alabama quarterback, Washington and Detroit pro, and eight-year assistant coach with Pittsburgh and the Minnesota Vikings. I say saddled because his interests, other than football, included the raising and keeping of horses, chewing tobacco, and wearing cowboy hats and boots. Well, *that* and all the lumps of sugar in Gilmer's cupboard wasn't what the doctor ordered to cure Joe Don Looney of his peculiar fetishes.

Anyway, getting back to the helmet business, after the scrimmage, Gilmer passed the buck again by asking linebacking coach Carl Brettschneider to see what he could do to make Looney wear one.

Carl went to Looney's room and charmed him into going to the training room, where Friday lined up five brand-new helmets for his inspection. "You can pick any helmet you want," said Carl. "That's because we miss you out there . . . and want you to play for us."

Looney selected one that fit his head. And then he tells Carl, "I really appreciate your help. And while we're at it, would it be all right if I had an extra pair of pants?"

A typical Looneyism—the sort of thing that went on while he played for the Lions. No question about it, he was in no way willing to submit to discipline. He had to be pampered and fawned over. And loved. Because he was able to get away with at least two of those incessant ambitions, it drove a deep wedge between Harry Gilmer and the ball club.

And yet, as I look back, I remember Gilmer as a fairly knowledgeable coach, and not a bad egg. His biggest fault was his fixation on reclaiming Looney for the world—at the expense of everybody else on the team. In the long run it cost him his job. I'm convinced of it.

Unchecked, and driven by his own dark, strange thoughts, Joe Don got into all kinds of scrapes. One made headlines. It happened in the parking lot of the Golden Griddle Pancake House in Royal Oak, a suburb of Detroit. There was a misunderstanding over who should pay the tab. Whereupon Looney tried to smash a beer bottle and use the jagged end to rip the other guy's face open. Fortunately, he was loaded to the gills and the bottle wouldn't break.

There were other things that only the players knew about. To illustrate. We were playing cards late at night in the dormitory. Looney came in with four girls—gigglers in short dresses and wooden shoes. They all went into his room, closed the door, and turned the record player on. There was an immediate uproar. Screams and grunts that sounded like a stampede of elephants. We kept playing cards. "Deal . . . Hit me once . . . twice . . . I'm pat . . . That fucking Looney . . . I've got two pair . . . three kings . . . a straight. . . . Take the pot . . . I can't concentrate. . . . Deal the fucking cards. . . ."

At one o'clock in the morning Looney opened the door and the girls giggled and wriggled their way out of the dormitory. "Ta-ta," he said, waving cheerfully.

John Gordy jumped up and hollered, "Ta-ta your ass! All that noise cost me thirty-two bucks!"

"God be with you," said Looney. Then he gently closed the door.

And there we were, old veterans with years in the game, sitting around for at least another hour, plotting ways to do the guy in without getting caught.

Another Looney classic. It happened the day he didn't even bother to show up for practice. Gilmer sent Joe Schmidt to his room to talk some sense into him. Joe Don was pumping his weights. Schmidt pulled up a chair and watched him for a while. Then he said, "The whole team would really appreciate it if you showed up for practice tomorrow."

Looney lifted a dumbbell from the floor, pressed it over his head, and said, "Aw, thank you, Joe."

"Well, yeah . . . I appreciate that. Anyway, I just want to tell you. I'm not bragging or anything, but I've been on this team for thirteen years. And in all that time I never once missed a practice."

"C'mon. You must be joking."

"I'm not. Honest to Christ."

Looney made a clucking sound and put down the dumbbell. "Joe, I think it's time you took a break. Listen, one day this week we can drive out to the country. I know a duck farm where we can sit and look at the ducks. And after that we can . . ." Schmidt left the room before Looney could finish the thought.

I'll close the book on Looney's one-year career as a Lion with this gem. We were in the middle of a tight game, and he was on the sideline when Gilmer decided to send him in with a play. "If they go into a four-four, tell Plum to use a thirty-three-sweep."

"Look, coach, if you want a messenger, call Western Union."

I can still see the unbelieving look on Gilmer's face—as I fell off the bench.

There's no explaining Looney. The day after Gilmer traded him to the Redskins, he was walking down Washington Boulevard in Detroit with Bob Tate, a local bartender. Suddenly, Joe Don looked up and said, "You know, I sure am glad I'm not a building."

Tate, not too impressed, said, "Yeah, it would be awful hard on you moving from town to town."

Not really. For Looney, traveling on the hidden roads of his own mind, life was kismet. Chance seemed to be the determining factor. But most pro players fall into another category. No matter the egos, or peculiarities, once camp opens and the game is at hand, the players sweat and curse, and absorb pain and fight off injuries, and go through the fires of hell in a thirst for acceptance. For them, the team is everything. They *must* belong. Everything else is secondary. Even winning. The fact is—win or lose—most players prefer to spend the length of their careers in one ball club. It's a rule of nature. As the saying goes: Good or bad, there's no place like home.

Sam Williams, for instance, practiced that axiom heart and soul. When he came to the Lions from Los Angeles in 1960, the trauma of new surroundings showed clearly on his face. He walked around for days in puzzled silence. I remember a road trip to Los Angeles, and Sam placing a call in the hotel lobby to one of his former teammates, saying how much he missed the friendships and everything else that had been part of his life the year before. Sam was a very emotional guy.

Then he made our team. And he made new friends,

and settled down. In a couple of years he became a starting defensive end, one of the best in the NFL. That suited him fine. Better still, he loved being a Lion. He thought it would go on forever, or at least until Father Time tapped him on the shoulder and handed him a monthly pension check. With that kind of thinking, Sam left himself wide open for a lot of kidding. And the victims of kidding usually are guys who are gullible. Sam was the most gullible guy I've ever known. I could sell him the Brooklyn Bridge, sand in the desert, water from the ocean; name it—I could sell Sam Williams anything.

In 1964 he banged up a knee in an exhibition game. Although he could still play on it, and perform up to par, every so often reserve end Bill Quinlan would be sent in to relieve him. A natural situation, under the circumstances. But Sam saw it as a threat to his job. "I'm okay," he'd tell me. "Coach should send me back in. We don't need Quinlan."

That's how it all started.

On our flight to San Francisco for the opening game of the season, I sat down next to Sam and said, "Let me tell you something. It's possible the coaches are thinking Quinlan can fill your position. They could be working on a trade right now. You never know in this business."

He says, "The sonofabuck is not good enough to take my place."

"That's what you say. The question is—what do the coaches say? I mean, you may be the greatest player in the world, Sam, but if they don't want you any-more, well, that's it."

In no time flat he's stewing like a prune. While he stewed, I moved out of the seat, gripped his shoulder, and said, "I hope you'll be coming home with us."

"Thanks, Al."

In due time, we played the 49ers, and had a nice edge with about two minutes to play in the first half. Up went the coaches' cry: "Substitutes!" Quinlan ran out to take Sam's place. Rookie Roger LaLonde ran out for me.

On the sideline, I said to Sam, "Quinlan plays the run pretty good."

"That dirty—"

"Now, Sam. I admit he doesn't rush the pass as good as you, but we've got three guys to do that. So where's our problem? It's against *the run*. And, like I say, Quinlan plays it pretty good."

Sam whipped off his helmet and threw it clear over the bench.

We played the second half and near the end of the game they pulled Sam again and sent in Quinlan.

"It's the last straw," he fumed as we lined up for the bus outside the stadium. "After all I've done for this team . . ."

"That's the way things are," I said. "Don't beef to me about it. Tell the coaches. I'm only a hired hand around here, just like you."

I kept giving it to him, and then second-string quarterback Earl Morrall—who's in on the mischief—started to work on him. "I had the same problem when I played in Pittsburgh," he's telling Sam. "After all I did for them, they got rid of me—just like that!"

Between Morrall and me, Sam's getting ready for a stroke. "What do those guys think I am?" he howled. "A piece of shit?"

We had the night off because we were staying on the Coast to play the Rams next. Morrall and I took Sam to dinner. He skipped the menu and ordered one martini after another. The more he drank, the more he thought about Quinlan. "What an ungrateful, rotten world this is," he said over and over.

Morrall finally put his knife and fork down, pushed back his plate, and said, "Sam, I don't think you'll be coming home with us. A trade is sure. Do you have any personal belongings we can take back to Detroit?"

By then, Sam's up to his eyeballs in martinis. He's had seventeen of them. Honest. Seventeen of those bombs. So he's feeling thoroughly confused, and he says, "Wha' c'n Ah do 'bout dish? Wha' c'n Ah do ..."

I said, "Sam, I'll tell you. If it was me, I'd make them pay for what they're doing. I'd go home. I'd leave and go home right now. I'd get on a plane for Detroit and stay there."

And Sam said, "Wouldjya ... really?"

And Morrall said, "You know Alex. That's what he'd do, Sam."

"Awright. Take me t'da airport. I think I'm gettin' sick."

The next morning he wakes up and the first thing he sees are the drapes in his bedroom. "Lois," he groans.

His wife tiptoes in. "You feel a little better, honey?"

"I don't know how I feel. How did I get here?"

Meanwhile, back in San Francisco, Morrall and I are doubled up from laughing so hard. But not for long. George Wilson blew sky-high when Sam called from Detroit. "What do you mean you can't remember how you got home!" Wilson screamed. "Get your ass back here on the next plane! And be prepared to pay for it—round trip!" Not only that, Wilson hit him with a $500 fine. Thank God he didn't suspend him. I don't think Morrall and I would've been able to live with ourselves if that had happened.

To ease our consciences—without letting on to how and why he came to all that grief over Quinlan—we had a big sign lit up outside the motel: WELCOME BACK, SAM.

21. The Bottom Line

It's February 1966. I'm vacationing in Miami with Joanie and our two kids. George Wilson, who's just been appointed head coach of the brand-new Miami Dolphins, meets me one morning in the hotel coffeeshop for breakfast. He says he's happy to be in the AFL. He also mentions that he's planning to buy a house—and needs a white rug for the living room.

I say, "There's a friend of mind in Detroit who's in the rug business. He sells all the name brands. Tell me what kind of fabric you want. And give me the dimensions. I'll get it for you wholesale." George is delighted. Then he asks if I'd be interested in joining the Dolphins.

"Gosh, I don't know. I've been a Lion so long. . . . Let me think about it."

A month later I'm at Peter Larco's restaurant in Detroit. Pete comes over to my table and says, "You have a call from George Wilson in Miami." I pick up. "Hi, George, anything wrong? . . . Oh . . . Well, there's been a strike at the factory. The rug will be shipped out in a few weeks. . . . Right, right . . . No, I haven't signed with the Lions yet. They keep coming up with the wrong numbers. . . . Yeah? . . . Wow, that's a tempting offer. Let me think about it some more. . . . Sure . . . Thanks, George. 'Bye."

In the middle of May, placekicker Pete Gogolak jumped from the AFL Buffalo Bills and signed a long-term contract with the NFL New York Giants. The AFL retaliated when commissioner Al Davis, in a stroke of genius, signaled his owners to start raiding the older circuit for established stars. A battle raged. Forty-niner quarterback John Brodie received a reported $750,000, four-year contract with the Houston Oilers. Quarterbacks Roman Gabriel of the Rams, Johnny Unitas of the Colts, and tight end Mike Ditka of the Bears were on the verge of jumping to other AFL teams. In June, the NFL was forced to its knees. The upstarts won. A merger of the two leagues became a reality.

During all that heat, I've been trying to get Russ Thomas, our new general manager, to boost my Lions contract from $25,000 to $35,000 annually. Now it's May 20 and I'm in Thomas's office arguing about my contract. "I've been All-Pro four times, same as tackle Merlin Olsen of the Rams," I remind him. "Olsen makes twice my salary. So I don't think I'm asking for something unreasonable."

"I'm not concerned about Olsen," says Thomas. "We're willing to give you thirty thousand dollars. That's the bottom line."

I tell him to go shove the bottom line. I would play out my option and go somewhere else the next year.

Okay. I return to my off-season job—selling used cars for Hoot McInerney at Northland Chrysler. I no sooner get my coat off when Russ Thomas calls me. In a tight voice, he says, "We'd really like to square away your contract."

I tell him, "There's nothing to discuss. We just went over it, for Chrissake. The bottom line—remember? There's no sense in continuing with this, Russ."

"I may have made a grave mistake. Let's start fresh, discuss it again—this time with Bill Ford."

"I don't know. I'll get back to you."

Immediately after I hang up on Thomas, a long-distance call comes in from Les Bingaman, who's now the Dolphin's line coach. "Hey, Al," he blurts out, "George Wilson's been trying to reach you all day. He even left his number at the Lions' office."

"What's up?"

"Something about a white rug. George says it hasn't been delivered yet. Say, are you in the rug business?"

"Not necessarily. Is George there?"

"No."

"Well, tell him the rug will be delivered next Wednesday."

We say good-bye. And a bell rings. *Ah-hah!*

Now I'm on the line with Thomas. "Hello, Russ. When can we get together?"

"Well, Ford won't be in until tomorrow...."

"Too bad. I'm flying out tonight. I have to talk to some people."

"Look, let's see if I can get in touch with him."

Thomas hangs up. Ten minutes later: *ring-a-ling-a-ling*. "Al, come down as soon as you can. Ford will see you. And we can get the contract straightened out."

William Clay Ford is behind his desk. Thomas greets me at the door with a firm handshake. Then Ford gets up and smiles benignly. I hear a typewriter going outside the office. Someone's typing furiously. "Have a seat," says Ford. We chat lightly, pleasantly. And I'm thinking: All these years . . . how they screwed me . . . Numbers whirl around in my head. *Big* numbers. Maybe if I ask for . . .

"Of course," says Ford, "we want to be reasonable about this. It's not as though we're strangers. You've been with us for nine years. A long time. And you've done a helluva job."

I clear my throat. "You're absolutely right, Mr. Ford. And I just want to tell you that I've enjoyed playing for the Lions. It's a fine organization. Nevertheless, I must now think of my wife, my children, and my future in football. And it certainly doesn't seem like my future is here."

"Alex, how can you say that?"

"With all due respect, sir, I have to work at three jobs in order to sustain myself and my family. Now I have to go elsewhere to see if I can make the kind of money I don't make playing in Detroit. I'm sorry. That's the way it has to be."

His eyebrows knot. "All right, Alex. Which team in the AFL wants you? Kansas City, Oakland, Buffalo ... Miami? Is it Miami? We *know* you've been talking to George Wilson."

"I don't have to discuss it with you. Whatever I'm doing has nothing to do with my relationships here."

"It has everything to do with us," says Ford. He walks over to the window, hands clasped behind him. The typewriter is still going. Thomas crinkles up a clown smile and waits for the boss to deal a trump card. He does. "We can piss farther than any of them," Ford says, still looking out the window. Then he turns around and smooths his tie. "How much do you need?"

The numbers crash together. An explosion. Come on, come on, think. Think! This is it! "Fifty thousand—cash!"

"All right. You have it. Now, what about the contract?"

Get ready, Bill Ford. Here it comes. "I think I need forty thousand a year for the next seven years. And no cut, no trade."

Ford nods. Thomas sticks his head out the door. "Helen, are you finished typing?"

They sign me in five minutes. And I'm out of the office.

Okay. Now I place a call to Miami. "Hello, George. I've got good news for you. The rug won't cost you a dime. I just made two hundred and eighty thousand dollars!"

"What did you do?"

"I signed a seven-year contract with the Lions."

"You dumb sonofabitch. You've underpriced yourself again!"

In July I turned thirty, and became a sort of elder statesman of the Lions when Harry Gilmer appointed me overall team captain.

Bull-necked, barrel-chested Joe Schmidt was captain for nine straight years. But he no longer had the urge to mix it up on the playing field. Two previous serious shoulder injuries hastened the decision. Before camp opened in 1966 he accepted the newly created position of linebacking coach.

Where had the time gone? I recalled a cold and windy autumn evening in 1965. Joe and I were driving along on the Edsel Ford Freeway toward downtown Detroit after the team had been beaten in Chicago. From the back seat, I heard him say, "I don't want to play until I can't stand up anymore. Maybe that's the way you feel, Al. But me . . . I want to quit while there's still some pride left."

"You can take being away from the game," I answered. "Football's my life. I'm going to stick around as long as I can, even if it has to be on the bench with a last-place AFL club. That's the difference between you and me."

Perhaps. Our backgrounds were certainly very much alike. Joe was born in Pittsburgh, the steel capital of the world. He grew up in a tough neighborhood, lost his father when he was young, and had an older brother who starred in high-school and college ball. The similarities made us natural allies.

When his chance came to be an assistant under Harry Gilmer, I told him, "Take the job, Joe. Sooner or later you're going to be head coach of this team."

I think I helped convince him that he'd be a good one.

Well, the 1966 season slowly marched to an end. Joe coached the linebackers, and I captained the full squad and played my usual game at tackle. Through it all, we stayed close. We talked a lot and thought alike on most every subject. Sometimes, while at home, I'd impulsively reach for the telephone. "Hello, Joe," I'd say, "I was just thinking that Gilmer should've . . ." And Joe would answer, "Me too."

On the subject of Harry Gilmer, we were of one mind. The man had a medieval way of doing things. He did them hastily, carelessly, and, oftentimes, stupidly. When he disposed of Nick Pietrosante shortly before the season got under way, nobody complained louder than Joe Schmidt. He told Gilmer it showed a complete lack of respect for Nick, who'd given seven faithful years to the ball club. "Well, he's all wore out—like an ol' horse," said Gilmer.

And Joe said, "That's your hangup, Harry. You don't know the difference between a football player and a horse."

Which illustrated Gilmer's essential failing. So I was bound to get into a dispute with him sooner or later. It happened in late October. At a Tuesday practice, he started to insult everybody on the field. "Awraht!" he threatened. "Whoever messes up from now on will be put on waivers, y'heah?"

I said, "Even me?"

"Tha's raht, Karras! Even you!"

I yanked off my helmet. "Let's get one thing straight, coach. If you have any complaints about the way I play this game, or the way I captain this team, take them to Bill Ford."

I went in and took a shower. And Gilmer went to Ford, who said, "Harry, Alex's contract is longer than yours."

To go on. There were a couple of false glimmerings in our losing season. In mid-November, Garo Yepremian, a pint-sized soccer kicker from Cyprus, booted a record six field goals against the Vikings, and we squeezed out a 32-31 win. The next week we beat the Colts at home. Then we dropped the last three games and finished sixth in the division.

It was the death knell for Harry Gilmer. In early January 1967, Bill Ford dismissed him as head coach and offered the job to Joe Schmidt. The players were thrilled. But Joe hesitated. "I have my family's future in my hands," he said. "I want to do what's best for all of us." Echoes of my own recent past.

Indeed, Joe loved his family very much. And he could afford to spurn coaching because his outside business interests netted him three times the money he earned as a Lion aide. There was an insurance business, a real-estate business, a manufacturer's rep business. Besides, he had recently made a nice profit selling his plush east side restaurant, the Golden Lion. And he was building a luxury home in Detroit's exclusive Birmingham suburb for his wife and five children. He wanted to spend his evenings there. He wanted to take weekends off, and take vacations with the family. Those were some of the factors that had to be weighed against a head-coaching life. Coaching would have him leave home in July for Cranbrook, spend eight weeks in training, devote long hours through a fourteen-game regular schedule from

September to December, participate in player draft and league meetings in January and February, and then make some out-of-town visits on club matters during the spring. Those were the facts, and Joe took all of them into consideration.

Intellectually, he turned to hearth and home. But within his soul, everything came from football: all truths, all lies, all dreams. So he went into Bill Ford's office and signed a contract for big money to coach the Lions for the next five years.

His baptism of fire took place on August 5, 1967, in Detroit's exhibition opener. To Joe's consternation, the Denver Broncos upset us 13-7 for the first victory ever by an AFL team over an NFL team.

We all felt like fools. A few of us played that way. In the second half, the referee threw me out of the game for kicking Bronco fullback Cookie Gilchrest in the stomach.

"You should've aimed for the nuts and immobilized him," Joe growled as I came off the field.

The damper was really on. And things didn't improve much as we pushed through the season. Still, the acquisition of rookies Mel Farr and Lem Barney gave us more bounce to the ounce.

Farr was our top draft choice, a six foot two, 210-pound UCLA prize package who produced the kind of running power that grabs headlines. He led the Lions with 860 rushing yards and was named NFL Rookie of the Year. I remember the day he ran 197 yards against Minnesota, one short of Hunchy Hoernschemeyer's club record. The shame of it is that all those yards didn't add up to a win. We were lucky to escape with a tie because of eleven record-breaking fumbles.

Lem Barney, a defensive back and punt specialist from Jackson State, was our number-two draft choice.

The moment Schmidt turned him loose in the opening game against Green Bay, we knew he was going to be a terrific cornerback. What moves! In all kinds of coverage—man-to-man, zone blitz, prearranged keys—Lem would be all over the receivers like Spanish moss, sweeping in from every which way to intercept passes, some for touchdowns. He ran three of them in during the season to tie a league record. And he won the NFL defensive Rookie of the Year award.

Mel and Lem. Spelled backward or forward, they still came out *Great*.

On the down side of things, our quarterback situation ran into a dead end. Milt Plum and Karl Sweetan took us there, so Joe decided he wasn't going to die with them. He started to call around the league for replacements. The Washington Redskins were willing to part with reserve quarterback Jim Ninowski. Joe wanted him in the worst way. His second choice was Bill Munson of the Los Angeles Rams. Either one, he thought, would make the Lions more respectable in 1968.

One night in December, Joe and I are having a beer at Lindell's. I can see that he's agitated about something, so I fish it out of him. "All right," he says, "if you really want to know, it's about my contract. It says I have a free hand to make trades. But Ford won't let me. What do you think of that?"

"I think it's terrible."

"You're damned right it is. I'm all set to complete a trade for Ninowski, and Ford says, 'Talk it over with Russ Thomas.' Which I do. And Thomas says, 'Let's wait for the college draft. We have a good shot at getting Greg Landry. He could be the next Bobby Layne around here. He could be our future.' Well, I tried to knock some sense into his head. I said, 'Russ, you're dealing with intangibles. Landry might be three or four years away from making it in this league. Can't you see that we need a seasoned quarterback to run the team—not a prospect?' He disagreed. He thought I was wrong. And I'm up a tree because Ford and Thomas outvote me two to one. It's a real disgusting situation, I want to tell you."

"What are you going to do about it, Joe?"

"I don't know. You have any suggestions?"

"Well . . . maybe you oughta resign."

There's a paralyzing silence. Then Joe sticks his chin way out and hisses, "What a dumb fucking answer *that* is."

I'm lucky he doesn't bite my head off.

The season closed and we finished with a lousy 5–7–2 record. When the 1968 college draft came up in January, the Lions selected Massachusetts quarterback Greg Landry in the first round.

About a month later sportscaster Al Ackerman of WWJ-TV in Detroit reported that Joe Schmidt offered to resign because the front office prevented him from making trades. Lyall Smith, our public-relations director, said the story was untrue. He claimed that Ford, Thomas, and Schmidt were in complete harmony on all trade matters. What a laugh! And when all the laughs died down, Joe stayed on as head coach.

Before the 1968 season opened Karl Sweetan went over to the expansion New Orleans Saints and Milt Plum was traded to the Rams for Bill Munson.

Meanwhile, Jim Ninowski, who should've been with us in the first place, remained in Washington as a substitute quarterback behind Sonny Jurgensen.

Not too long after Al Ackerman's exclusive on Joe's beef with the Lions' front office hit all the

papers, WWJ-TV terminated Ackerman's services
and went right on selling air time to the Ford Motor
Company.

Go figure it out.

22. There's No Business Like . . .

George Plimpton is a very unusual writer. For example, if he wanted to write about a bullfight, he'd really get into the bullfighter's head. I mean, Plimpton would learn everything he could about him, including his gut reaction to the fight itself. Next, he'd put on a silk shirt and velvet pants, carry a red cape and a sword into the arena, and then parade around with a rose between his teeth while twelve guys got ready to shove an old asthmatic bull into the ring. Then Plimpton would fight the bull. It's his *shtick*. He's been doing things like that for years, facing old bulls, major league hitters, professional prizefighters, pro football linemen, Ping-Pong players, and so forth; doing the same kind of things athletes do for a living. Only Plimpton does it as a writer.

He's one of the best around.

I first met him in Detroit, the year of my suspension. He was writing a book called *Paper Lion*. What he did was go out to Cranbrook disguised as a draft choice from the Newfoundland Newfs. Then he had himself placed on the Detroit roster as a rookie quarterback, and got away with it for a few days. When the guys finally caught on they didn't raise a stink. As a matter of fact, they enjoyed having him around because he was willing to undergo a full regimen of training without asking for special privileges. So he fit

in. He became one of them. And it all came to a good
end.

He played quarterback in one series of the big intrasquad scrimmage at Pontiac Stadium, almost played
in the team's first exhibition game against the New
York Giants, and left Cranbrook with enough
material to write *Paper Lion*. It has since become a
classic in sports literature.

For whatever it means, Plimpton saw fit to include
me in the book. Some of his "Alex Karras tales" were
picked up from the players and coaches. The rest he
got from me over at Lindell's A.C. He'd come in lots
of times and we'd talk until the wee small hours. At
first, I couldn't understand a word he said. He used
words as if he had invented the dictionary. He delved
into mysterious topics, such as philosophy and anthro-
pology and *sex*. His wisdom stretched to the outer
limits. It flew right over my head. But I hung in. And
found him to be charming, witty, and quite likable.
There was within him a sensitivity toward what I
happened to be going through during that year of ex-
ile. He refrained from getting into any questions
about my suspension unless I wanted him to. So we
became friends. And through the years we've stayed
close. Fact is, my fourth child is named after him:
George Plimpton Karras.

During the 1967 season, Plimpton contacted me. He
had just sold his book to the movies. A fellow by the
name of Stuart Millar would be producing *Paper Lion*
in association with United Artists, and he'd be using
players in principal parts. I'd be one of them,
Plimpton said.

For days after, I walked around dreamily, staring
into mirrors, imagining myself as a great big movie
star. Bigger than Clark Gable, Tyrone Power, Paul
Newman. Bigger than any of them. Damn right. I had
always been interested in acting, at least ever since I

killed the audiences at Emerson High in the Spice and Variety musicals. I felt I could do it. And Tony Frank was a big influence. After college, he had gone to New York to be an actor. Every now and then, in the late 1950s, I'd see him on television, playing small parts in shows like "Naked City" and "The Untouchables" and "Playhouse 90." When that happened, my heart jumped. The early days came dancing back and I remembered how it used to be when Tony and I would stand in front of the old Roxy Theatre on Broadway, looking intently at the marquee, with Tony saying, "My name's going to be up there someday." And there he was on television! Acting! And getting paid! I wanted to kiss the screen. I was so happy for him. One day I got a letter from Tony. He was in Hollywood, studying to be a director. When the Lions played in Los Angeles, I'd go out to his apartment and we'd talk about his film projects. Sometimes he'd break out a script and we'd act out different parts, and Tony would say, "Gee, Al, you're good. You should be working in films."

"Yeah. Sure. So long, Tony. See you.

By Christ, I was going to play pro football for the next *thousand years*. Who needed acting?

I met Stuart Millar at the London Chop House in Detroit on a fall morning in 1967. We had eggs Romanoff. "Mah-velous dish," he said between bites. "Perfectly mah-velous." Millar wore a beret, and a flaming yellow ascot hung loosely around his neck. After we finished eating he reached into his satin-lined inside jacket pocket and produced two dark-brown cigars, obviously expensive Havanas. "In the words of Kipling," Millar purred as he lit mine with a solid gold lighter, " 'A woman is only a woman, but a good cigar is a smoke.' Wouldn't you agree?"

"Rah-ther, Stuart. Here—here."

I was playing the role of an act-or, loving every minute of it.

Contemplating all things, and contemplating nothing, I sat and listened as Millar talked about the *Paper Lion* production schedule. Most of the winter filming would take place at a private school in Boca Raton, Florida. A veritable paradise, he said. Palm trees, a swimming pool, delightful weather—all this and more awaited if I'd agree to terms. "I'm quite certain we can arrive at a satisfactory figure," he was saying. "Do you have one in mind, Alex?"

"Oh . . . I think the proper *remuneration* should be ten thousand dollars, plus all expenses, of course. And, naturally, I would like to rent a Honda while I'm down there."

"Yes—well—very good. You've just made yourself a deal, m'boy. I look forward to having you with us in Boca Raton."

"Jesus Christ, Stewey, when does the plane leave?"

Millar hired Alex Marsh to direct the picture. A nervous, very peripatetic guy, with a three-pack-a-day cigarette habit. He was always enveloped in fumes. As a true lover of the arts, Marsh simply could not fathom the inner world of pro football. Sometimes it would take him hours to round up the Lion players to do a scene "What's wrong with you people!" he'd shout. "Can't you take directions?" If one of us laughed, or farted, or—God forbid—cursed, Marsh would throw up his hands and scream, "I'm dealing with animals! Animals!"

My very first scene—the first one of my life before a camera—was an exchange of a few lines of dialogue with Alan Alda, a New York actor who had been signed to play George Plimpton. It went beautifully. Smooth as silk. Marsh was flabbergasted. And everyone on the set called me "First-take Karras."

The name stuck, but somehow the takes got longer.

In a barroom scene, in which a whole bunch of us were happily getting drunk, Alda joined in to prove he could lift his glass with anyone in the joint. He drank an awful lot of beer—a beer a take—twenty-seven in all. On the last take he threw up on the bar, then slid to the floor like a decked whale. The scene was thrown out. We had to start all over again the next day. This time Marsh cut it down to three takes to prevent Alda from getting cirrhosis of the liver.

In the same scene, Alex Marsh the director decided to be Alex Marsh the actor. His role: a barroom antagonist, a surly civilian fed up with the game of pro football and especially Alan Alda. Marsh was supposed to call him a fraud, Alda was supposed to get angry, and the players were instructed to grab Alda before he had a chance to beat up on Marsh. That's the way it was blocked out before the cameras rolled. What we did—we waited until Marsh said his lines, then we threw beer all over him and held him upside down by the ankles. "It's a zoo," he gurgled, "a bloody zoo . . ."

One other memory of those carefree days in Boca Raton. A CBS-TV sportscaster and crew of technicians came down to film a brief segment for one of their programs. While John Gordy and I stood by, the sportscaster asked Marsh to comment on some of the things that particularly pleased or displeased him while directing the Detroit players.

"Oh, we get along fine. It's a big, happy family. All of us are striving to make *Paper Lion* a memorable film, perhaps the best of its kind since *Pride of the Yankees*. So, I'm very pleased. There are no problems."

Now John Gordy is waved in by the CBS director to say a couple of lines. He's holding his blazer over the shoulder—Sinatra-style. On cue, Gordy ingenuously supports Marsh's "togetherness" speech and steps back.

"Cut."

My turn. I walk into the scene and say to Gordy, "Put your coat on, you fucker."

Marsh went completely insane. He started to scream and yell, and the cameras followed him all the way out to lunch.

The world premiere of *Paper Lion* was held in Detroit. With the floodlights going, with people jammed against the ropes, with television and radio reporters interviewing co-stars Lauren Hutton and Alan Alda, plus a supporting cast of Detroit Lions "actors," it became one of the most thrilling experiences of my life; unlike the sense of excitement I had felt while running onto a playing field before an important ball game. This was different.

I went in and settled in my seat, prepared to enjoy what I was about to see up there on the screen. I wasn't disappointed. Nor was the audience. They laughed throughout the picture. There were cheers and whistles at the end. When the lights came up, total strangers made a special effort to grab my hand and say, "A great performance. Congratulations."

So I said to myself—maybe I should pursue this after my football career is over.

For some, the long season of youth had already passed.

Listen: A boy grows tall, his limbs become firm, muscles harden; the entire body churns with power. Now he is a man. A unique man capable of achieving over and above what is expected of lesser men. So we cast his image in stone and metal and we call him *immortal*.

But look! A thousand and more Man of the Year trophies are turning green in pine-paneled dens across the land. And the angry winds howl in the eaves, and the ice is heading south again, and on some near-distant day the tallest mountains will slide into the oceans and disappear.

Are we all fools, dreamers, or what?

It's hard to tell.

In 1968, the long season of youth had already passed for Jim Taylor, Ray Berry, Sam Huff, Lenny Moore, Lou Groza, Don Chandler, and Jim Ringo; star players who produced imposing statistics to embellish their names. I knew them all. And suffered inside when they left the game. But there were still plenty of years left in me. Hell yes. I felt that the old legs could run on and on and on and on. So I went back to Cranbrook.

Before long, the only thing that mattered was the season ahead.

I hardly remember it. There was one game, though. The game we lost to the Philadelphia Eagles in Detroit on Thanksgiving Day. I remember the rain, the mud, the quagmire. And Sam Baker, with those high shoes. He kicked four field goals against us, which put him in second place in all-time scoring behind Lou Groza. It gave me a feeling of participating in history. I remember that. And something else. I didn't do anything wrong all day. When they tried to run my hole I plugged it, making nineteen or twenty personal tackles. So I remember that, too.

The rest of it is a formless knowledge of stadiums, locker rooms, hotel lobbies, movie houses, bars, buses, planes. The planes carried us to Dallas, Green Bay, Minnesota, Chicago, Los Angeles, Atlanta, and Washington. The planes brought us back home and we played Chicago, Green Bay, San Francisco, Baltimore, Minnesota, New Orleans, and Philadelphia. The sequence doesn't matter. We had a season. The record shows we lost more than we won.

If the losses had me down, Hollywood shot me up the clouds for winning a dramatic role in the "Daniel Boone" television series.

The big, bright moment came. There I was, sitting in at a script session at the Twentieth Century-Fox Studios, reading dialogue as if I had been trained for nothing else. When the session ended, I asked one of the veteran actors, "Do you know who the director will be?"

He gave me a Jack Benny stare, then said, "Yeah, he's the guy who directed *How Green Was My Valley*."

Movie trivia was my meat. "You mean the one with Walter Pidgeon and Roddy McDowall . . . and Donald Crisp? That one?"

"Mm-hm."

"My God, that picture was made back in the thirties. The director must be a very old man by now."

"My friend, he's not only old, he's had six heart attacks in the last two years. He could go at any minute."

"Oh, Jesus. I better not get him upset. What time are we supposed to show up on the set?"

"Six-thirty tomorrow morning—promptly."

"Okay. What scene?"

"Scene one."

"Thanks."

I cabbed to my hotel in Beverly Hills, ordered up a pot of coffee, and started to read scene one. I even read the dog's dialogue. I knew exactly when the dog was going to bark. By the time I fell asleep, scene one was completely committed to memory.

Not another soul was on the set when I arrived at six-thirty the next morning. At seven, the makeup girl came in. Then the actors. At eight o'clock I was all made-up and in full regalia. Then I saw the director. He sat in his chair like the High Lama of Shangri-La; an ancient bag of bones holding a megaphone in one hand while the other hand shook and twitched on his lap.

"Quiet on the set!" went up the cry.

"Scene two!" the director rasped through his megaphone.

Someone threw me behind a door. Someone pointed at me. I opened the door, walked out; and said, "Hummahummahumma . . ."

"Cut!"

A couple of assistants helped the director out of his chair. Everybody took a thirty-minute break. I looked around for the actor who had laid all the wrong information on me. He was nowhere in sight.

Well, I learned my lines for scene two during the break and gave a pretty good account of myself. When it was over, the old director got out of his chair unaided and kissed me on both cheeks. Later in the afternoon, I learned that my actor friend had once been a regular in the series, but, for one reason or another, fell into disfavor and had been reduced to playing occasional bit roles. When I saw him the next morning, I didn't have the heart to ream him out. I felt sorry for him.

Show business. It was getting to me, flowing into my system like vintage wine into a Frenchman's stomach. My head began to swim with a real "high" of giddy excitement. For twenty years I had little interest in anything other than The Game. The game was it.

Not anymore. Now a fresh trail had opened, and I made up my mind to follow it as far as it would take me.

But there were seasons still to play. In the summer

of 1969 I put on my football gear and once again threw muscle and sinew against the blocking sleds at Cranbrook. I ran laps around the field with the old bunch. I razzed the new kids who had come in from Florida and Arizona State and Youngstown and California and Utah State: Jim Yarborough, Larry Walton, Craig Cotton, Dan Goich, and Altie Taylor. Those were the new names. There were more who didn't stick around. It was the same old grind.

We started in Pittsburgh. We were beaten. We came on against New York and Cleveland and Chicago. . . . And so it went. As always. The games went on and I went on. And then, at Lambeau Field in Green Bay, I was scissored in the line by Packer guard Gale Gillingham. He caught the right knee and ripped the ligaments. There was a hot, sticky throb of pain. It bubbled up and grabbed at my throat. A sob escaped. Then I sank down. A whistle sounded. A circle of players formed and crowd noise rushed in from everywhere, getting louder and louder. It held, then slowly lowered to a disturbing hum. The bastards are waiting for me to die, I thought.

"Get away! I'll make it on my own." I boosted myself up. The sideline seemed a mile away, but I hobbled toward it, listening all the while to a thunderous blast of hatred that charged through the stadium and rattled over my head. It was the sweetest sound of all. An ovation! The greatest of my pro career. I had tormented the Packer fans long enough. They were happy I got hurt. They were glad to see me go. I was proud of those creeps. At least they told the truth.

In the overall scheme of things, we had a good year, the best since 1962. It still didn't get us any higher than second place, as the Minnesota Vikings, led by quarterback Joe Kapp, clinched the Western title and made it to the Super Bowl.

In the winter, they operated on my knee. The ligaments were repaired. I had to wear a cast and get
around with a cane. So patterns changed. Priorities
shifted. I kept in touch with Tom Vance, who ran a
successful advertising and promotion firm in Beau-
mont, Texas, and was also a director of public rela-
tions for the National Football League Players
Association. He had taken over the management of
my show-business activities the year before. I'm sure
he was sent to me from heaven.

Here was a man who believed I had something to
offer besides football talent. He got me booked on all
the big talk shows: Johnny Carson, Merv Griffin,
Dick Cavett, David Frost. He lined up a string of banquet dates. I made as much as $3,000 an appearance
through Tom's efforts.

I'll never forget the banquet I did with Joe Louis.
We had been signed to work six of them as a team. In
all my introductions, I would say, "And now, ladies
and gentlemen, the fabulous, the wonderful, the leg-
endary Brown Bomber—let's hear it for the former
world heavyweight champion . . . Joe Louis!"

There'd be a great roar and a ten-minute standing
ovation. Then Joe would get up and say, "Ah wanna
thankya fer comin' down here tonight . . . Ah lak
y'all . . . and Jack Dempsey wasn't that bad. . . ."
And he'd sit down. Another ovation. Then the
master of ceremonies would say, "And now the main
speaker, Alex Karras." The crowd would look at each
other and say, "Who the hell is he?"

I didn't mind it. I'd talk for an hour, mixing humor
and straight football talk, finally getting the audience
to enjoy my routine. But the fact that Joe Louis never
spoke one word to me during the entire banquet
swing—that hurt.

We had one more to do in Canada. This time I dispensed with the usual pleasantries. I waited for the

proper hush. Lowering my voice a full register, I said, "Ladies and gentlemen, when I was a small boy in Gary, Indiana, my greatest dream was to grow up to be the heavyweight champion of the world. You see, I had someone to emulate. That man was Joe Louis. Everything he said, I believed. Because he was so terrific. Now, Joe used to sell a drink called Joe Louis Punch. It was a chocolate pop, and I would drink gallons of it every week. [I turned to Louis.] Joe, I just want to say this. Your chocolate pop gave me a million pimples. It was the worst pop I ever drank in my life. It changed my attitude about boxing, Joe. And especially about you. The only one who saved me from being scarred for life was Tony Zale, the ex-middleweight champ. One day I saw him on television . . . doing an Ex-Lax commercial. And because he comes from my hometown, Joe, I went right out and bought some Ex-Lax. And I shit all your pop away."

Screams.

After I sat down, Joe Louis said to me, "Ah lak y'all. What's yo' name?"

23. Yassah, Massa

I had three years to go on my Lions contract. Now, in the summer of 1970, I reluctantly reported to camp.

An extended series of talks with owner Bill Ford, general manager Russ Thomas, and head coach Joe Schmidt got me nowhere. I would have to stick by the contract. There would be no pay increase. Not a dime more. And that was final. Well, they had a right. I was tied and bound in servitude to the Lions' organization, and so was everybody else on the team.

Sure, salaries were rising dramatically in professional sports. The Joe Namaths of football, the Rick Barrys of basketball, the Hank Aarons of baseball, and the Bobby Hulls of hockey were already in the seventy-percent tax bracket, or getting close. But they were the team showcase models, polished like diamonds by club owners and set before the admiring crowds who were only too willing to pay for the right to see the superstars in action. However, it was an entirely different matter with the semistars of pro sports. As long as they wanted to play the game, they had to jump to the owner's tune.

Take Lem Barney. He had gone to every Pro Bowl since coming to the Lions as a rookie in 1967. And yet he was only making $15,000 in 1970, his option year. I knew that as a fact. John Gordy, then the National Football League Players Association president, showed me the figures. I was shocked. Besides that, Gordy confided, Russ Thomas promised Barney a $10,000 bonus if he went to the 1969 Pro Bowl. He did. And Thomas reneged on his promise. What could Barney do? What could any of us do? Under the Rozelle Rule, we didn't have a chance to break from our bonds. The rule, in effect, said that a player could not quit and play for another team. And it also said that a player had to report to his team with or without an agreement.

I attacked the windmills. I told Thomas I wanted to have my final three years' pay compressed into two years, which would give me $52,500 a season. He laughed it off. "Impossible. We have a contract. You have to stick to it." All right. I then asked for a twenty-five-percent "cost of living" increase.

"You have a contract . . ."

With that, I took off for my in-laws' home in Iowa. Three or four days before camp opened, Joe Schmidt called. "You're hurting the team," he said. "You're setting a bad example for the younger players."

"Joe, if it's that bad, trade me."

Nothing happened. So I called Russ Thomas. "We don't want to trade you," he said. "And I will not, under any circumstances, change any provision in your contract."

On August 7 a group of reporters converged on me in the Cranbrook locker room. They asked about my running fight with the front office, which had been well publicized. "Trade?" I said. "What trade? I love it here. I love Bill Ford. I love Russ Thomas. I love Joe Schmidt. I don't want to go anywhere." Yeah. And the blacks didn't want to head north before the Civil War, either. Dey jes *loved* bein' slaves. Yassah, massa.

I took my whipping like a man. There were no outward cries of pain when Joe Schmidt took away my job as defensive captain.

For twelve pro football seasons my passions had been like a nerve that the world jarred against. Now, at thirty-five, the knife-edge urge for battle has subsided. I can feel the relaxing of muscle, the slight but significant slowing of bodily movement. Time is catching up. I'm thirty-five, and ready for a last go-round. Maybe this season. Maybe next. But no longer.

The damaged knee, though restored to normal use, is still tender. Trainer Kent Falb tapes it once a week to keep the fluid from building up. In the scrimmages, I take some hard whacks on it. No problem. So I get into the chute, ready to go full out at the bell.

"Monday Night Football" came to Detroit for the first time on October 5, 1970. The American Broadcasting Company telecast our contest against the Chicago Bears, and we put on a good show, licking them 28–14. But the better show, from what I heard and read the next day, went on upstairs in the ABC booth. Howard Cosell, "Dandy" Don Meredith, and Keith Jackson were at the mikes, mixing Shakespearean oratory, corn-pone witticisms, and straitlaced reporting into a fun-filled TV package that hit jackpot percentages in the ratings game.

I first met Howard Cosell in 1957. I was in New York, preparing to sail to Athens for the Balkan games. He was just breaking into television, and came to my hotel room for an interview. He seemed unsure of himself; fidgeted and smoked and said very little while we waited for the equipment to be set up. But once he got on camera, he handled himself superbly, with great assurance, in a relaxed, cool manner. He pulled more information out of me than I would've thought possible, so it didn't turn out to be just another interview. For me, it was an education.

Anyway, Howard made it to the top by stirring up things in sports; by telling it like it is, and sometimes like it's not. Sometimes he's completely outrageous on the air. Sometimes his ego gets in the way of sound judgment. And sometimes he gets overly involved with certain athletes I don't respect. But that's okay. I'm sure there have been times when he couldn't understand some of the things I said and did while working with him on more recent "Monday Night Football" games.

It takes all kinds—so they say—and Howard is most definitely one of a kind. While others fed pabulum into their microphones and typewriters, he was giving the people real issues to think about. So, inevitably, quite a few of his peers started to blast him. They said he was a phony, an irresponsible muckraker, and worse. I don't buy any of it. Not for an instant. He doesn't genuflect before the owners of ball clubs. He's not condescending to superstars. He tries to give the lesser-known athletes some recognition if their talents deserve it. And that's more than I can say about a lot of guys who have been covering the sports scene since I've been in it. Yeah. I've had enough of those "Gee whiz, honest-to-God, folks, Johnny Unitas—no kidding—goes to the bathroom . . ." broadcasters and writers. Give me Howard Cosell, anytime.

The show goes on.

On November 8, 1970, we played the Saints in New Orleans, and had a 17-16 edge with two seconds to go. In trotted Tom Dempsey, the Saint kicker, to try a 63-yard field goal. All the Lions started laughing. To us, it was as ridiculous as the time Bill Veeck sent a midget to the plate as a pinch-hitter for the old St. Louis Browns.

The Saints lined up and their center snapped the

ball. We didn't put on a rush. We just ran around on our side of the scrimmage line and took positions from where we could get a good view of the kick—and we kept laughing. Then Dempsey dug his toeless right foot into the ball, and we turned and watched it. And the ball sailed along, end over end. And we laughed and laughed. Not one of us stopped laughing until the official in the end zone put his arms straight up.

Tulane Stadium erupted; a tornado of fans roared onto the field, and Dempsey got buried under a debris of well-wishers. An unforgettable moment in pro football history, and I was there.

Crowds. I've always enjoyed them. To me, they're grandstand performers, no less involved than I've been as a playing performer. To wit: Before the Chicago Bears moved over to cavernous Soldier Field, they played all their home games at Wrigley Field, where the stands are so close to the gridiron you can hear what everyone is saying. Well, in 1960 I became acquainted with a delightful character who regularly attended all the Bear games at Wrigley Field. He sat in a box seat on the third-base side, directly behind the Lion bench; a heavy, moon-faced man of Japanese ancestry, with a voice that sounded like a kamikaze pilot making a bomb run over Pearl Harbor. The first thing I heard as I emerged from the dugout to start warming up was this Japanese fan. The words cracked over my head.

"Hey, Kallus! You horseshit!"

So help me, he would keep it up from opening kickoff to the final gun; year after year. And I loved it. But I never let on.

Finally, in 1970, I decided to introduce myself to the guy. In the Lions' farewell appearance at Wrigley Field, I came out of the third-base dugout and, on schedule, the same old kamikaze yells sliced through the wind.

"Hey, Kallus! You horseshit!"

I immediately hopped over the fence, went directly to this box seat, stuck my face right up to his, and growled, "Didn't I kill you in Korea?"

In the last five weeks we played four first-place teams and beat them all. Then we went into a playoff against the Dallas Cowboys.

The day was sunny. There was a rookie Dallas back named Duane Thomas; smooth and graceful, yet he ran for 135 rough yards and reminded me of a faster Jimmy Brown. There was a Dallas field goal in the first quarter. In the fourth quarter Greg Landry was sacked for a safety. So Joe Schmidt lifted Landry and put in Bill Munson, who got us back in the game. He took us down to their 29-yard line. Then an interception—a tipped pass off the fingertips of Earl McCullouch into the hands of Dallas cornerback Mel Renfro. It ended our last hope for a championship. The whole team was heartbroken. Sick.

But what remains more vividly, while thinking of my last full year in pro ball, is the drastic change that came over Joe Schmidt. He began to do the same things as a coach that used to drive him livid as a ball-player. He became an object of resentment. Those of us who knew him in earlier times—playing exuberantly and working conscientiously to become a ten-time All-Pro—now saw a man who had fallen into the same rut as Harry Gilmer. Now the assistants ran the ball club, as before. They trapped Joe into judgment blunders, and, drugged by indecision, he listened and reacted to their likes and dislikes, no matter how petty.

Our own friendship started to cool when Joe didn't back me during the spring and early-summer contract negotiations with Bill Ford and Russ Thomas. It left scars. We couldn't speak openly to each other after that. But I did what I always did; I busted my tail for him, pushed as hard as ever to help the team win ball games.

For the truth of it, I also set the record straight about my partnership in Lindell's A.C. bar. It came through an interview with *Sport* magazine writer Lou Prato, who got into the subject of my suspension, and his understanding that I had to sell my interest when ordered by Pete Rozelle.

"I kept it five more years," I said.

Prato's mouth flew open. "How'd you manage *that*?"

"It was a verbal thing. Nothing went down on paper. Hell, no. If Rozelle had put in writing that something illegal was going on at Lindell's, he'd have been slapped with the biggest lawsuit he'd ever seen."

"Well," said Prato. "You did tell Rozelle in 1964 that you sold your interest. Were you lying?"

"Lying to whom? To a guy who's trying to screw me? I don't give a damn what Rozelle says."

At that point in my life, no man in the whole world could tell me what to do.

24. Even Big Guys Cry

I don't know if anyone else has food problems in Mexico, but my stomach rebels whenever I go down there. It seems like those little Mexican amoebas wait for me at the border and as soon as I cross over the line they jump on me and stay with me until I leave the country.

So what do I do? I sign a contract with Hannah-Barberra and fly to Mexico for a dramatic role in a television western called "The Hard Case." Of course, I bring along a portable john for any and all emergencies.

On the first day of shooting I say three lines, then head for the john, and I come back to say the next three lines. And so on. I say thirty lines the first day.

On the second day they saddle up some horses for an action scene. Apparently the horses aren't too well fed in Mexico, because all of them look very scrawny. Mine looks as though he should be riding me instead of the other way around. Anyway, the actors get on and we snake along a narrow path to the top of a high cliff. The footing is extremely precarious. The horses have to be good—or else. So here we are, with me in second position behind Clint Walker, the star of the movie.

"Action!" shouts the director.

The horse behind mine suddenly rears back—and the rider goes over the cliff into the ravine below.

"My God, that's one helluva stunt man!" I shout to Clint Walker.

Pale as a ghost, Clint says, "Unfortunately, Al, he's not a stunt man. He's one of us."

I immediately begin looking around for my portable john.

A few weeks later I'm back Stateside, and call the director. He says the actor has recovered, but won't be riding any more horses for Hannah-Barberra.

In the spring of 1971 Joe Schmidt and I talked about the coming season. He wanted to know if I intended to play. I said, "Sure. My legs are really strong. I'm going to have a good year."

When training camp opened, he asked me if I had changed my mind, shifting his eyes down as he spoke. I was used to this kind of behavior. He hadn't looked me straight in the eye for the past three years.

I said, "Don't expect too much at first. I plan to come on slow. Then I'll show you what I can do."

"Fine. That's exactly what we want."

It's the last time we talked about my playing.

I played for a limited time in our exhibition opener against the New York Jets in Tampa, Florida. Same thing when we met the Cincinnati Bengals at home.

At Ann Arbor I put in more time against the Baltimore Colts, taking on bruisers like Dan Sullivan, John Williams, and Bill Curry, slipping past them now and then to jam the runners. Overall, I thought it was a respectable outing.

A week later, off to Miami. The Dolphins gave me a real going over. I knew it. Nobody had to tell me.

Against the Buffalo Bills at home, I shuttled in and out of the lineup, taking one good lateral shot at O. J. Simpson as he came around on a sweep. And I made a few tackles. Meanwhile, none of us could get a solid pass rush going. It was one of those days: hit and miss.

On Sunday, September 12, we got ready to play our final pre-season game against the Eagles in Philadelphia.

Our Veterans Stadium locker room filled with the sound of laughter, whistling, quiet talk; players stripped and hung up clothes, put on pads and uniforms, tied shoelaces, and wriggled into helmets. Lion hearts and minds become one. On the field above, a lingering dream of games and seasons would go on for many. For some, the dream would end.

Nick Eddy came in to dress for the game; ready to play as much as his knees would let him. He injured them in 1966, the year he became Most Valuable Player of Notre Dame's undefeated national championship team. Taking everything into account, the Lions picked him in the second round of the college draft as a future. He arrived at Cranbrook in 1967, but his knees were still bad, so he didn't play. The next season Eddy ran the ball only forty-eight times for 176 yards. A year later, seventy-eight times for 272 yards. Then, in 1970, he was used on special teams before a hand injury removed him from the active roster.

Those are the statistics; very little else. What it doesn't show is, Nick Eddy worked harder than anyone I know to make it big in pro football. That he didn't is not his fault, for there's no team sport played anywhere in the world in which the occurrence of knee injuries is more frequent than in American football. In one study, 350 former University of Missouri football players responded to a questionnaire, indicating that 105 had sustained knee injuries, and 37 had had surgery performed. Well, Eddy's number came up at Notre Dame. And he couldn't overcome his crippled condition with the Lions. But he tried. Oh, how he tried.

Now he's among us in the Veterans Stadium locker room, looking this way and that.

"Where's my locker? I don't see my name tag," he says to no one in particular.

Trainer Kent Falb calls him aside. They're close enough so that I can hear Kent say, "Didn't Joe Schmidt tell you . . . ?"

"Tell me what?"

"Oh . . . Well, he cut you this morning. I'm sorry, Nick. I'm really sorry."

Nick was devastated. With Schmidt's approval, he had stayed over an extra day for therapy, then took the morning plane out to join us in Philadelphia. Now this.

Seeing him slumped down on a stool, shading his eyes to hide the sorrow and shame, I smack an open palm against the wall, then go to find Joe Schmidt in the coaches' office.

I explode. "You didn't have to do it that way!"

"What the hell are you talking about?"

"Nick Eddy! He busted his hump for you. He put everything he had into being the kind of team player you say you've always wanted. And look what happens to him! Goddamnit, Joe, you cut him off like an old cleat. You didn't even have the decency to tell him!"

"Well, I was going to . . ."

"Whatever you were going to do, Nick had to hear it from the trainer!"

I slam the door in his face, and then go out to play football.

And hook up, nose to nose, against Mark Nordquist, the Eagle guard. He's young, tough, durable. From start to finish it's a real slugfest. I have the edge. I keep dropping him in his tracks, forcing him to blink away the dizziness. Seven or eight times I ride over his jersey to get at the quarterback. Three times it helps to produce interceptions. The groan of fan disappointment is music to my ears.

We walk off the field with a 49–10 victory. I figure it's all mine.

I flew to New York the next morning, and the following evening I appeared on the Johnny Carson show, doing football bits—locker-room fables and foibles—some off the top of my head. I went over big.

After the show I took a cab out to La Guardia Airport to catch a late flight back to Detroit. One of the ticket agents at the desk said, "You have a telephone message."

I dialed Joe Schmidt's number. "Joe? What's happening?"

"I hate to tell you this, but we placed you on waivers today."

"You what? Aw, c'mon . . . you're kidding."

"No, Al. I don't think you can do the job anymore."

Unbelievable! There was no mention of the years played, the awards won, the services rendered. Hell, no. Just a few mumbled words of regret, and me hanging up in total shock. I went into the lounge and had a drink. To shut off Joe Schmidt's voice. To forget what he had said, what he looked like, what he once meant to me. A while later, staring into an empty glass, I wanted to cry. But big guys aren't supposed to. So I found myself laughing until it hurt; laughing idiotically to keep from bawling like a baby.

That night, driving out to my home in Bloomfield Hills, I snapped the radio on. The news of my firing was all over the dial, including a statement that Joe had given to one of the local sportscasters:

"The decision on Karras was the toughest I ever

made. Once we were close, personal friends. And once he was the best defensive lineman I'd ever seen in Detroit."

You're damned right, Joe. On both counts.

Joanie met me at the door, the look on her face telling me that she knew. We went into the living room and watched my taped performance on the Carson show. After that we talked.

I said, "What really burns me is that they did it after thirteen years—and that way. I heard it on every radio station all the way home."

"What difference does it make?" she answered. "From now on, you're a free man."

About the Author

Herb Gluck is a contributing editor to *The Associated Press Sports Almanac*. He is the author of *While the Gettin's Good* and *Baseball's Great Moments*.

Super Sports Books from SIGNET